BUILDING A BUSINESS

on

FAITH

How Faith and Resilience Can Guide Your Business Journey

By

CARL B. JOHNSON

BUILDING A BUSINESS ON FAITH

How Faith and Resilience Can Guide Your Business Journey

To my mother, who taught me to work with what I have and make it work.

To my father, who showed me a world beyond the city and reminded me never to let anyone define who I am.

To my son, whose resilience inspires me to keep pushing forward, even when the odds are stacked against me.

And to all my friends who have stood by me through every wild idea and venture, lending an ear and encouraging me when I needed it most—thank you for your unwavering support.

CONTENTS

PREFACE

When I first felt the nudge to build a business anchored in faith, I wasn't entirely sure how the journey would unfold. I knew I wanted to serve people and honor God's principles, but the path ahead looked both exciting and uncertain. This book is the result of those early steps, the lessons I learned as I combined faith and business in a real, everyday way.

In these pages, you will see that this venture isn't just about earning money or chasing success. It's about a deeper calling—using your talents, showing resilience, and shining light into the marketplace. Each chapter focuses on a key theme, from overcoming doubt and celebrating small wins to reflecting on how God guides us in tough decisions. You will find stories, practical tips, and gentle reminders that faith can shape every corner of our work.

You do not need to be a seasoned entrepreneur or a spiritual expert to benefit from these insights. My hope is that whether you are just starting out or have many years of business experience, you will feel encouraged, refreshed, and equipped. If you are unsure how faith connects with pricing, marketing, or leadership, know that you are not alone. We will walk through those questions together, discovering how a faith-based approach can spark creativity and kindness in all our dealings.

Above all, I pray these chapters leave you with fresh courage to pursue your mission. May the tools and stories here inspire you to keep going— even when challenges arise. And may you remember always: you are never alone in this journey of building a business grounded in principles that last. Faith guides you, and there is grace enough for every step ahead.

PART I

LAYING THE FOUNDATION

01

THE POWER OF BELIEF

"And without faith it is impossible to please God,
because anyone who comes to Him must believe that
He exists and that He rewards those who earnestly
seek Him."

(HEBREWS 11:6)

A Seed of Hope

You hold a special kind of power inside your heart. This power can help you build a strong business. It can also lift you up when times feel hard. This power is called "belief." Belief is what happens when you decide that something is possible. Even if you cannot see it yet, you trust that it can come true. This is not just about wishing or dreaming. It is about knowing deep inside that good things are on the way.

Imagine a small seed. When you plant a seed in the ground, you trust that a plant will grow. You might water it, make sure it gets sunlight, and wait patiently. You do all this because you believe in that seed's power to sprout. Your faith in the seed is like your faith in yourself or your business. You believe that with the right care and time, your goals will bloom into reality.

Belief is a gift that keeps you moving forward. It helps you stay brave when you face a scary challenge. It gives you strength when you feel weak. You might have days when you wonder if things will ever work out. On those days, hold tight to your faith. Remind yourself that big dreams often start with small steps. When you truly believe in your business idea, it shines through everything you do. People notice your confidence. They see that you are serious about your vision.

I remember when I started my first business. I was 16 years old and was selling computer repair services. I felt excited, but I also felt nervous. I did not know if anyone would buy from a kid with little to no experience in sales not to mention I didn't have a store front or a company phone – just a BMX bike and a bus pass that I would use to make house calls. In my heart, though, I believed that could help people and I believed I was going to be successful. I prayed about it every day. I wrote down my goals. I made simple plans and followed them. Little by little, good things began to happen. My belief was the spark that started the fire and before I knew it I was receiving orders from everyone in north Philadelphia. Without belief, I would have never taken the first step.

In this chapter, you will learn about the power of belief. You will see how it can guide your actions and fill you with hope. You will discover ways to make your belief stronger and more steady. You will also learn why belief matters so much when you decide to start or grow a business. By the end of this chapter, I hope you feel inspired to trust your journey. I hope you feel ready to plant your own seed of faith and watch it grow.

<u>Remember, you are not alone.</u> Many people have walked this path before. They, too, had doubts. They, too, faced storms. Still, they chose to believe in something bigger than their fears. You can do the same. Let your belief be a safe harbor when life gets tough. Let it be your anchor when you feel lost at sea. If you hold on to that belief, you might be amazed by how far it can take you.

What Is Belief?

Belief is more than just a thought. It is a deep feeling that something is real or true, even if your eyes cannot see it yet. Sometimes, people call it faith or trust. When you believe in your business, you are saying, "I know my idea can help someone. I know it can grow into something special." This does not mean you ignore problems. It means that no matter what happens, you keep hope alive.

Think of belief as a friendly light that guides your path. When you look ahead, that light shows you the way. It tells you that you can make it. This light does not remove the rocks or twists in the road. But it makes the journey less scary. You know you have the strength to face whatever comes next.

Many people struggle with belief. They might say, "I hope this works," but deep down, they are afraid. They worry about failure. They think, "What if I try, and nothing happens? What if people laugh at me?" These thoughts can dim your light. They can make it hard to see your bright future. That is why growing a strong sense of belief is so important. You want your inner light to shine, even on cloudy days.

One way to check your level of belief is to ask yourself, "Do I really think this idea can succeed?" If your answer is "yes," you already have a strong seed of belief. If your answer is "I'm not sure," do not worry. You can still nurture that seed. Sometimes, our hearts want to believe, but our minds are scared. In those times, you can say short prayers or repeat helpful statements. You can say, "I am strong. I am able. My business can help people." When you do this often, you water the seed of belief.

Belief is also about trusting a power bigger than yourself. For some people, this power is God. For others, it is a sense of the universe or a higher purpose. Whatever it is for you, belief means you trust that you are not alone. You trust that you can get guidance and help, even when you do not see how it will come. You trust that your path has meaning.

Why Belief Matters in Business

Your belief is like the engine of your business. It keeps you moving forward. When you believe in what you do, you do not give up easily. You keep trying, even when it feels tough. People around you notice this. They might think, "Wow, she really loves her product," or "He truly believes this idea can help." That kind of energy is catching. It makes people want to support you.

When you believe in your idea, you also become more creative. You look for new ways to solve problems. You do not get stuck, because you trust there is a solution waiting to be found. You become like a brave explorer who will climb any hill to find a better path. Without belief, you might turn back at the first sign of trouble. You might say, "This is too hard," and walk away. But with belief, you say, "I can keep going. I can find a way."

I have seen this in my own life. I remember a time when my business was not making enough money. Bills were piling up, and I felt scared. Part of me wanted to quit. But another part of me said, "No, I believe this business can still work." I prayed for wisdom. I asked friends for advice. I tried new ideas, like changing my advertising plan. Slowly, things began to turn around. If I had given up when it got hard, I would have never known how close I was to success.

Belief also helps you face criticism. Not everyone will support your dreams. Some might say, "That will never work," or "You are wasting your time." These words can hurt. But if you truly believe in your idea, you can stand firm. You can say, "I respect your opinion, but I have a different view." You can keep going, even when others doubt you. Eventually, some of those doubters might become believers, too, once they see your progress.

In business, there are many ups and downs. You might have a great sales month, then a slow one. You might hire someone who turns out to be a perfect fit, or you might make a mistake in who you hire. Through it all, a strong belief will keep you steady. It will help you learn from mistakes instead of getting stuck in them. It will remind you that every challenge is a chance to grow.

Seeing Possibility Instead of Problems

Problems are part of any business journey. You will face things like tight budgets, limited time, and stiff competition. Yet, when you believe, you do not let problems block your view of what is possible. Instead, you see them as puzzles to solve. You might even welcome challenges because you know they help you become smarter and stronger.

Imagine you are looking through a camera lens. If your focus is on problems, that is all you see. You notice every tiny issue, and it starts to feel too big to handle. But if you shift your lens toward possibility, you start to see the hidden doors. You notice how a problem can spark a new idea or lead you to a new solution. That shift in focus is powered by belief.

I recall a time when I had trouble reaching new customers. My sales were flat. I felt stuck. I could have thought, "I guess my business has hit a wall." Instead, I believed there was a way to grow. I just had to find it. So, I tried different ways to connect with people. I started hosting small in-person and online events to show them what my product could do. One day, a person who came to an event ended up telling her entire church group about me. Soon, I had many new customers. If I had only seen the problem, I might have given up. But my belief helped me see a possibility hiding right behind the problem.

When you see possibility, you also become more joyful. You realize that each problem is a chance to learn something new. You stay curious instead of frustrated. You might ask yourself, "What can I learn from this?" or "How can I turn this around?" Those questions spark hope. They remind you that you are the person in charge of your attitude. Yes, you may not control everything that happens, but you control how you respond. When you choose a hopeful response, you stay closer to your goals.

Nurturing Your Belief Daily

Belief is not just a one-time choice. It is something you build and maintain each day. Think of it as a garden that needs water, sunshine, and care. If you forget to tend your garden, weeds will grow and choke your plants. In the same way, if you forget to nurture your belief, doubt will creep in.

A simple way to grow your belief is by starting each day with a few minutes of quiet. You can pray, meditate, or just breathe deeply. During this time, speak encouraging words to yourself. You can say, "I am capable. My work is worthy. I trust that today will bring new opportunities." These positive words act like water for the seed of belief. They keep your mind focused on what is good.

Writing down your goals is another great way to keep your belief strong. When you see your goals on paper, they feel more real. It is like drawing a map for your journey. Each time you read your goals, you remind yourself where you are headed. If you add pictures or drawings that match your goals, that can help even more. For example, if you dream of opening a small bakery, you could draw a picture of a happy customer enjoying your pastries. Looking at that picture can spark a warm sense of possibility in your heart.

Reading uplifting books or listening to encouraging messages can also grow your belief. Sometimes, you need to hear stories about other people who overcame hard times. Their stories remind you that success is possible. They show you that many journeys start with a spark of faith. If they could do it, maybe you can, too.

Finally, do not forget to celebrate each small victory. Did you make one new sale today? Did you get a nice review from a customer? These small wins feed your belief. They show you that you are moving in the right direction, even if the steps are small. Over time, many small steps lead to big results.

Turning Doubt into Determination

Doubt can show up at any time. It might sneak in when you face your first major setback. It might whisper in your ear, "Maybe you are not good enough." It might say, "Maybe your idea is too small." Doubt can be loud, but it does not have to control you. You can learn to turn doubt into determination.

One way to fight doubt is to ask, "Is there any real proof that I cannot succeed?" Often, you will find that there is no proof—only fear. Fear tries to convince you that you will fail before you even start. But if you believe in a power greater than fear, you can quiet those dark thoughts. You can remember that everyone who ever succeeded felt doubt at some point. They chose to keep going anyway.

I remember when I tried to create a new product line. It felt like a big stretch. I worried that my customers would not like it. But I also felt excited because I believed in the product's value. Doubt still whispered, "Do you really think you can pull this off?" But I turned that doubt into determination by working extra hard on my idea. I tested it, asked for feedback, and improved it. When I finally launched it, the product did better than I ever expected. That feeling of victory reminded me that doubt is just a test. If you push through, you grow stronger.

Turning doubt into determination also means seeking help when you need it. If you are stuck, find someone who can guide you. This can be a mentor, a friend, or even an online group of supportive people. Share your worries, but also share your vision. When you speak your dream out loud, it becomes more real. Others can encourage you and help you see a clear path forward.

The Role of Faith in Belief

Faith often goes hand-in-hand with belief. Faith is like trust in action. It says, "I will move forward, even if I cannot see the end." In business, this is powerful. You trust that your efforts will pay off. You trust that there is a plan for your success, even if you have to wait. Faith does not mean ignoring reality. It means you keep hope alive while facing the truth.

Many people find faith through a relationship with God. They pray for guidance and strength. They ask for wisdom in making decisions.

They also give thanks for the good things that come their way. For some, faith might take a different shape, such as a belief in the universe, or a sense of purpose that goes beyond just making money. Whatever shape your faith takes, it can be a steadying force.

When you have faith, you do not feel alone in your journey. You sense that help can come from unexpected places. You might meet someone who gives you the perfect advice at just the right time. You might stumble upon a new idea while talking to a friend. These moments feel like small miracles. They remind you that you do not have to figure everything out on your own.

I have experienced this many times. Once, when I was stressed about a business loan, I prayed for clarity. The next day, I met a kind banker at a community event. He explained a new loan program that fit my needs perfectly. That meeting felt like an answer to prayer. Of course, I still had to do my part and fill out the forms. But my faith and belief helped me see that solutions were possible.

Belief in Yourself

Having faith in your product or service is important, but you must also believe in yourself. You need to trust that you have what it takes to learn, grow, and become better each day. Sometimes, people think they are not smart enough or talented enough to run a business. They might say, "I wish I could, but I am just not cut out for that." This is false. Your abilities can improve with effort. Your knowledge can grow with study. Belief in yourself is what helps you put in that effort without giving up.

Look back on your life. Think about times when you did something you once thought was too hard. Maybe it was learning to ride a bike or play an instrument. At first, you felt clumsy and uncertain. But with practice, you got better. In business, it is the same way. You might feel scared or unready, but you can learn. You can improve by reading, taking classes, and watching how others succeed.

When you believe in yourself, you also become kinder to yourself. You learn to forgive your mistakes and move on. For example, if you try a marketing idea and it fails, you do not call yourself a failure. You say, "I learned what does not work. Now I can try something else." That is a powerful mindset. It keeps your spirit open to new ideas and helps you stay motivated.

I remember feeling very shy about public speaking. As my business grew, I had to speak at workshops. I felt nervous every time. But I believed I could improve. I read books about public speaking. I practiced in front of a mirror. I asked friends for honest feedback. Over time, I became more comfortable. Now, speaking to groups is one of my favorite things to do. If I had never believed in myself, I would have stayed stuck in my shell.

Sharing Your Belief with Others

Belief is not just something you keep inside. It is also something you can share. When you speak about your business with passion, people can feel your energy. You can spark excitement in others. They might think, "I want to be part of this vision." Sharing your belief helps you find customers, partners, and supporters who connect with your purpose.

When you talk to someone about your product or service, let your genuine belief shine through. You do not have to exaggerate or use fancy words. Just be honest about why you believe your business can help. Speak with clarity and warmth. People often remember how you make them feel more than the exact words you say.

Also, remember that you can share belief with people who are just starting on their own journey. Maybe you meet a friend who wants to open a small shop. They feel nervous, and you can tell they are unsure. You can encourage them. You can say, "I understand how scary it can feel. But I believe you can do it. I started off feeling scared, too, and look where I am now." Those words might mean the world to someone who is feeling alone.

I once mentored a younger business owner who wanted to start a tutoring service. She was worried no one would sign up. I told her how I felt the same way when I began. I shared my story of passing out flyers and talking to people at community events. Over time, her service grew. She always tells me that my belief in her gave her the courage to keep going. Sometimes, all it takes is one person who believes in you.

Real-Life Experience—My Leap of Faith

I want to share a deeper story from my own life to show you how belief works in action. There was a time when I felt stuck in a job that did not bring me joy. Every morning I would hit the snooze button over and over again regretting having to go to work. I had a small dream in my heart to start a cybersecurity consulting business. But I was afraid. I worried I did not have enough money saved. I worried about what people would say if I failed. Then, one day, I felt a strong nudge to step out in faith. It was as if God was saying, "Trust me. Take a chance."

I prayed hard about this decision. I wrote down my fears and then wrote down how I could face them. For each worry, I asked myself, "What is the worst thing that could happen?" After listing my fears, I realized that my worst-case scenario was not as bad as I thought. Even if I failed, I could learn something valuable and try again. This gave me enough courage to set a date to leave my job.

The first few months were hard. I had to work long hours to find clients. But each time I felt tired or afraid, I reminded myself of why I started. I believed in my mission to help people grow their businesses. I believed that I had a gift for teaching and encouraging others. I kept that belief close to my heart.

Slowly, my consulting business began to pick up. I booked a few small contracts. Then, a client recommended me to a large company. That company hired me for a bigger project. From there, my reputation grew, and more people came my way. I saw how my faith and belief had carried me through the scary parts. It felt like walking across a shaky bridge, but each step of faith showed me the bridge was stronger than I thought.

Looking back, I am so grateful I chose to believe. If I had let fear rule me, I might still be stuck in that old job. I would have missed out on all the wonderful clients and friends I have met through my business. Now, I can look others in the eye and say, "You can do this. I know because I did."

Let Your Belief Lead the Way

Belief is a powerful force that can light your path through any storm. It helps you see possibilities where others see problems. It keeps you steady when doubt tries to shake you. It gives you hope, even when the road is long. When you believe in your vision, your product, and yourself, you become a beacon of light for others, too.

Remember that belief is something you tend every day. You do it by feeding your mind with positive thoughts, by setting clear goals, and by trusting in a power bigger than your fears. You keep your heart open to new ideas and new solutions. You share your faith with friends and strangers. Over time, your belief will grow from a small seed into a strong tree with deep roots.

In your business journey, there will be ups and downs. That is natural. But each challenge is a chance to grow stronger in your faith and skills. Each trial teaches you something new. Your belief will help you rise above every obstacle. It will help you discover answers that others miss, because you are looking through the lens of hope.

You have a purpose that only you can fulfill. Your business idea is special because it comes from your heart and your experiences. When you mix that idea with strong belief, you create a force for good in the world. People will see your determination. They will feel your passion. This is how you inspire trust, loyalty, and respect.

As you move forward, keep this chapter's lessons close. When fear knocks on your door, answer it with faith. When doubt whispers in your ear, replace it with uplifting words. When you face problems, turn your focus to possibilities. And when you feel tired, remember why you started in the first place. Let your belief guide you step by step, and trust that you are on the right path.

This is the power of belief. It is the key that opens many doors. It is the light that keeps you going in the dark. It is the seed that grows into a mighty tree. May your belief be strong and steady as you continue your business journey. May it fill you with hope, courage, and the joy of knowing that the best is yet to come.

02

PRINCIPLES OF SPIRITUAL ENTREPRENEURSHIP

"Commit your work to the Lord, and your plans will be established."

(PROVERBS 16:3)

Balancing Spirit and Business

You have a dream to build a business that is successful, but also guided by a higher purpose. You want more than just making money. You want to serve others, grow as a person, and feel connected to something bigger than yourself. You might call this force God, the Universe, or simply your spiritual path. Whatever you call it, you feel it in your heart. It pulls you forward.

When you decide to let faith guide your business, you become a spiritual entrepreneur. This means your choices and actions are not only about profits. They are about living by core values. You trust that when you help others in good ways, blessings will flow back to you. You believe that business can be a tool for love, growth, and positive change in the world.

In this chapter, you will explore key principles of spiritual entrepreneurship. These ideas can help you stay true to your values while building a lasting company. You will learn about cause and effect, the power of trusting divine timing, and the importance of loving service. You will see how spiritual teachings connect with everyday business tasks like marketing, planning, and hiring. By the end, you will understand how to blend faith and work in a way that honors your soul.

I remember the first time I felt a stirring in my heart to start a business. I was excited about the idea of being my own boss, but I also wanted to stay true to my spiritual beliefs. I prayed for guidance. I wanted my business to feel like an extension of my faith and not just a way to make money. Over time, I learned many lessons about how to keep my spiritual core strong. My business grew when I acted with love and kindness. It struggled when I forgot my deeper purpose.

In the pages ahead, I will share some of these lessons. You will see how each principle connects to daily life. You will learn ways to put these principles into practice, even if your resources are small at first. You will also find comfort in knowing that you do not walk this path alone. Many entrepreneurs before you have invited God—or their sense of a higher power—into their work. They have seen miracles happen when they keep their hearts open to divine guidance.

Defining Spiritual Entrepreneurship

Being a spiritual entrepreneur means you run your business with heart and purpose. Yes, you still focus on earning a profit, but it is not the only thing you care about. You also care about helping people and honoring your values. You see your customers as more than sources of income. You see them as people with hopes, struggles, and goals of their own.

When you are a spiritual entrepreneur, you treat your team members with respect. You pay them fairly. You give them chances to learn and grow. You also try to create a product or service that truly benefits others. This does not mean you ignore the need for revenue. A spiritual entrepreneur knows that profit is important for keeping the business alive. But profit is not the sole driving force.

In many ways, spiritual entrepreneurship is about being mindful. You do not rush into decisions without thinking about the bigger picture.

You take time to pray, meditate, or reflect before making big moves. You ask, "Is this choice aligned with my values? Will it serve others in a good way?" These questions keep you anchored. They remind you that success is not just about numbers. It is also about inner peace and moral integrity.

A key part of defining spiritual entrepreneurship is realizing it is a journey, not a destination. There is no moment when you suddenly become the "perfect" spiritual entrepreneur. You keep learning as you go. You make mistakes, but you keep your heart open to growth. You keep seeking a deeper relationship with God or your higher power. You also give yourself grace on days when everything feels difficult.

When I began to see my business as a spiritual practice, I noticed a change. I became more patient with myself and with others. I started to see customers as partners in a shared mission. I felt more joy and less stress because I knew I was not alone. I was part of something bigger than my single company. This sense of connection gave my business new energy.

The Law of Cause and Effect

You might have heard the phrase, "You reap what you sow." In simpler words, what you put out into the world comes back to you. This is the law of cause and effect. It says that your actions create results. When you act with love, honesty, and kindness, good things tend to return your way. When you act with greed or dishonesty, you might gain something for a while, but it usually does not last. Negative actions often lead to negative outcomes down the line.

In spiritual entrepreneurship, you pay close attention to the causes you create. You try to plant seeds of goodness. You take time to treat your customers fairly, even if it means a smaller profit in the moment. You go the extra mile to ensure your product is of high quality. You speak kindly to your team, even on stressful days. These are the seeds of kindness and integrity you sow each day.

Over time, these seeds grow into a harvest of blessings. Your customers trust you, so they stay loyal. They recommend you to friends. Your team respects you, so they work with joy. They come up with fresh ideas because they feel safe sharing them. Money might come a little slower at first, but it comes steadily and with fewer problems because the root of your business is solid.

Of course, the law of cause and effect also works if you make harmful choices. If you treat people like tools, you might make quick money, but you lose their respect. If you cheat customers, you might see a short burst of profit, but negative reviews will follow. This creates a ripple of bad will that can hurt your reputation. Eventually, the business crumbles because it lacks a stable foundation.

I once worked with a business partner who cared only about quick wins. He did not mind bending the truth to close a deal. At first, it seemed like he was succeeding. Money rolled in, and people praised him for his confidence. But soon, unhappy clients began to complain about unkept promises. The business faced a wave of refunds and lost trust. In the end, he had to close shop. That experience taught me how important it is to honor spiritual principles, because the law of cause and effect never fails.

Trusting in Divine Timing

Sometimes, you might have a big business dream. You do all the right things: you plan, you work hard, you network. Yet, success does not show up when you expect it. This can feel frustrating. You might question whether your dream is worth pursuing. But as a spiritual entrepreneur, you learn to trust divine timing.

Divine timing means believing that things happen when they are meant to, often for reasons you cannot see. It means being patient when results are slow. It also means staying open to sudden opportunities that appear out of the blue. Sometimes, you wait months for one good client, and then three arrive in the same week. Other times, you experience a slow season that allows you to rethink your business strategy. Later, you realize this break was necessary for your growth.

When you trust divine timing, you still take action. You still do your part to move forward. But you also let go of the need to control every outcome. You do not force things before they are ready. You do not panic if things take a little longer than planned. Instead, you watch for signs and nudges that guide your path.

I remember trying to launch an online cybersecurity course for my business. I spent weeks creating videos, writing content, and setting up a WordPress website. I was so excited. But when I launched it, I got very few sales. I felt crushed. I prayed and asked, "Is this dream not meant to be?" Then, a few months later, I was invited to speak at a large event (till this day I have no idea how they found my website because our SEO was terrible). Many people at that event loved my ideas and asked if I offered an online course. I was able to share the same course I had built earlier. Because of that event, my course sold well, and I met new clients. In that moment, I realized the timing was just not right when I first launched. I needed to wait for the right audience. Trusting divine timing taught me to keep working, keep believing, and stay patient for doors to open.

Serving Others with Love

Love might seem like a soft word in a business setting, but it is actually very powerful. When you approach your customers, clients, or team members with love, you want the best for them. You offer products or services that truly help. You listen carefully to their needs. You solve problems, not just to earn more money, but to create real change in their lives.

People can sense when you genuinely care about them. This sense of caring builds trust. It sets you apart from others who might see customers only as dollar signs. When people feel loved or appreciated, they tell their friends about you. They become repeat customers who are excited to see your business grow. Love, in this sense, becomes a key part of your marketing strategy, even though you do not do it just for that reason.

Serving with love does not mean letting others walk all over you. You can still have policies that protect your time and resources. However, you make these policies in a way that is fair and respectful. You explain them clearly and kindly. When someone has a complaint, you respond with empathy. Sometimes, you might offer refunds or do extra work if it is in line with your values. At the same time, you do not allow people to take advantage of you.

In my own journey, I noticed that when I truly cared about people's well-being, my business became more joyful. I did not dread calls or messages from customers. I looked forward to hearing from them, because each new conversation was a chance to help. I remember one customer who had trouble using our service. Instead of blaming him, I listened closely to his struggles. We found a solution that worked better for him, and he stayed loyal for years. That is the power of love in business: it creates loyalty and goodwill that no amount of advertising can buy.

Aligning with a Higher Purpose

Every business has a purpose beyond just making money. It might be as simple as bringing people tasty treats (like a bakery), or as grand as helping solve world hunger. As a spiritual entrepreneur, you recognize that your higher purpose is tied to serving humanity and honoring the divine spark within yourself and others. You think about the positive change you can bring to the world.

When you align with a higher purpose, you become more passionate about your work. You wake up with a sense of excitement because you know you are not just selling products. You are contributing to something bigger. This sense of purpose fuels you on days when you feel tired or discouraged. It reminds you that your work matters in ways that go beyond a bank account.

You can also share your purpose with your customers. Let them know your mission. Maybe you donate a part of your profits to a charity that fits your values. Maybe your product itself has a meaningful impact on people's lives. When customers see that you care about more than money, they become part of your mission. They feel good about supporting you because they know they are helping a cause they believe in, too.

I used to sell handmade gifts, and part of the money from each sale went to a local children's center. I told customers, "When you buy this item, you are also helping kids in need." Many people loved this idea. They were happy to pay for something that served a dual purpose: it brought them joy, and it helped someone else, too. Over time, I realized my higher purpose was to use my business to spread hope and kindness. Even when sales slowed, I stayed motivated because my work had a deeper meaning.

Balancing Profit and Purpose

One challenge for spiritual entrepreneurs is balancing profit with purpose. You may ask, "If I truly care about people, is it wrong to charge high prices?" or "How do I stay fair to my customers while also paying my bills?" These are good questions. The truth is, it is possible to make money and still keep your values intact. In fact, financial success can allow you to do even more good.

Think of money as a tool. If you use it wisely, it can support your mission. You can pay fair wages to your team. You can invest in better materials or technologies that serve your customers. You can donate to causes you believe in. The key is to remember that money is not your ultimate goal—it is a resource that helps you live out your mission more fully.

Still, you must be careful not to lose sight of your spiritual principles in pursuit of profit. If you find yourself cutting corners on quality to save a few pennies, that might be a sign that your focus has shifted away from service. If you start to see your customers only as numbers, it might be time to pause and realign. A spiritual entrepreneur stays aware of these temptations. They check their heart regularly, asking, "Am I still serving with love? Do my actions honor my values?"

I once struggled with pricing my products. I worried that if I charged too much, customers would think I was greedy. But I also knew I needed to earn a living and pay my team. After prayer and reflection, I realized I had to price my services at a fair rate that reflected their true value. I explained to customers why I set the prices. I talked about the quality materials I used, the labor costs, and the charitable donations. Many people understood and were glad to support a business that aimed to do good with its profits. In this way, I learned that profit and purpose can live side by side.

Creating a Spirit-Led Team Culture

Your team is a vital part of your business. As a spiritual entrepreneur, you want your team members to feel respected and inspired. You hope they bring their best selves to work and believe in the company's mission. To make this happen, you should create a culture that reflects your spiritual values.

First, lead by example. If you treat customers with kindness, your team learns to do the same. If you handle mistakes with patience and honesty, they see how to solve problems without fear. Show them that you value compassion, fairness, and open communication. Celebrate small victories and encourage people to keep growing.

Second, invite your team to share ideas and feedback. Let them know their voices matter. When you include them in important decisions, they feel a sense of ownership. This can lead to fresh insights and more loyalty. You can also hold short meetings to discuss the company's purpose and values. Remind everyone that the business exists for a higher reason than just profit.

Third, be mindful of each person's individual gifts. Some team members might be great at customer service, while others are better at handling finances. Help them develop these talents. Offer training, support, and chances to move up. By supporting their growth, you invest in the future of your business in a way that also honors their personal dreams.

I once hired someone who was shy but incredibly kind. She struggled with sales calls because she was not very outgoing. However, she had a real talent for writing heartfelt emails. She could connect with customers in a genuine way through written communication. Instead of forcing her to make phone calls, I reassigned her to email outreach. She thrived in that role, and our email sales grew a lot. This experience taught me that part of spiritual leadership is placing people where they can shine.

Using Spiritual Wisdom in Everyday Decisions

Sometimes, people think spirituality is only for Sunday mornings or quiet retreats. But a spiritual entrepreneur knows it can guide everyday business decisions, from hiring to pricing to choosing the best vendor. You do not have to make these decisions alone or rely only on logic. You can pray, meditate, or reflect each time you need clarity.

For instance, if you have two potential suppliers, you might do your normal research first—comparing prices, checking reviews, and looking at quality. Then, you take a moment to quiet your mind. You can ask, "Is this supplier aligned with our values? Do I feel a sense of peace when I think about working with them?" Trust the wisdom that comes from your intuition and spiritual guidance. Often, the answers become clearer when you open your heart to listen.

You can apply this to hiring as well. Of course, you review someone's resume and check their references. But you also pay attention to how you feel when you speak to them. Do they seem excited about your mission? Are they respectful and honest? Sometimes, a person looks great on paper but does not mesh well with your team culture. Other times, a candidate might have fewer skills but a genuine passion and a teachable spirit.

Spiritual wisdom also helps you plan for the future. When you create a business strategy or set goals, you might start with what is realistic. But you also leave room for faith. You ask, "What does God (or the Universe) want to do through this business?" You dream bigger than you might dare to on your own, because you believe in possibilities that go beyond human limits. This does not mean you stop doing the hard work. It means you combine practical steps with trust in a higher plan.

My First-Person Experience—A New Beginning

I want to share a personal story of when I truly felt the power of spiritual entrepreneurship. Years ago, I was running a small cybersecurity company. I was hungry for business, so I took on any client who would pay. It did not matter if there needs directly matched our services. I just wanted to be successful.

Over time, I felt uneasy. Some clients sold items that went against my core beliefs. Others treated their customers poorly. But I kept working for them because I was afraid of losing income. My stress levels rose, and my passion faded – it now turned into the same job I kept hitting the snooze button. I knew I was not running my business in a way that honored my faith.

One day, after a difficult call with a client who demanded look the other way after knowing they were running an unethical business, I decided enough was enough. I prayed, "God, show me how to do business in a way that pleases You. I don't want to compromise anymore." I felt a sense of peace telling me to let go of the clients who did not align with my values. This was scary because it meant losing a chunk of revenue. But I trusted that if I acted from a place of faith, I would be provided for.

I ended contracts with three clients who clashed with my morals. At first, my monthly income dropped. I questioned if I had made a foolish mistake. But within a few weeks, I got an unexpected call from a well-known nonprofit. They wanted help with a big marketing project.

They said they had heard good things about my work. Suddenly, my schedule filled with new, value-aligned clients who needed my skills. These projects were not only financially rewarding, but also personally fulfilling.

That moment changed my entire outlook. I saw firsthand that when you run your business by spiritual principles, doors open that you cannot predict. It felt like God was rewarding my obedience and clearing a path for better opportunities. Even though it was risky, I learned that faith is often about taking bold steps, believing that help will come when you do what is right.

Practical Ways to Put These Principles into Action

Now that you have read about these principles, how do you use them in daily life? Here are some practical ideas:

Start Each Day with Reflection or Prayer

Take five minutes each morning to center yourself. Ask for guidance and wisdom for the day ahead. You can also read a short devotional or uplifting quote that inspires you to lead with love.

Write a Values Statement

Write down your top five values for your business. For example: honesty, kindness, service, growth, and gratitude. Post them where you can see them each day. Use them as a filter for your decisions.

Share Your Purpose

Tell your team or customers why your business exists. You might say, "We believe in empowering families," or "We strive to make the world greener." This reminds everyone—including you—of the deeper reason behind your work.

Do a Daily Kindness Check

Each evening, think about how you showed kindness during the day. Did you take time to listen to a worried team member? Did you treat a difficult customer with compassion? Even small acts make a big impact.

Trust Your Gut

When faced with tough choices, do your research, but also trust your intuition. If something feels off or against your spirit, pause and pray about it. Look for a path that aligns with your faith.

Give Back

Consider ways your business can serve the community. You might donate products to local charities, sponsor an event, or volunteer your time. This is a tangible way to practice spiritual entrepreneurship.

Practice Gratitude

Keep a small notebook and write down three things you are grateful for in your business each day. This habit shifts your focus from stress to blessing.

Stay Humble

Remember that success is a gift. Share credit with your team, give thanks to your higher power, and stay open to learning. Avoid letting pride push you off your spiritual path.

Seek Guidance from Mentors

Find people who share your values. Learn from their experiences. Ask them how they balance profit and purpose. You might gain insights that save you from making avoidable mistakes.

Celebrate Small Wins

Take time to notice each step forward. Even if it is just a single new customer or a kind note from someone who loves your product, let it fuel your faith. These small victories add up to bigger success over time.

Walking Forward in Faith

When you choose spiritual entrepreneurship, you invite a sense of peace into your work. You trust that you are guided, supported, and loved by a power greater than yourself. You still face deadlines, tough decisions, and market shifts, but you handle them with a calm heart. You know there is a bigger story unfolding, and your business is part of it.

These principles—cause and effect, divine timing, serving with love, aligning with purpose, humility, and gratitude—act like a compass. They keep you on track when temptation, fear, or doubt tries to lead you astray. They remind you that your business is not just yours; it is also a vessel for blessing others. When you lose sight of these truths, you can always come back through prayer, reflection, and intentional action.

As you move forward, remember that you do not have to do everything perfectly. Spiritual entrepreneurship is a journey of growth. You will learn along the way, make new discoveries, and correct mistakes. Each day, you have a chance to deepen your faith and refine your approach. Each day, you can ask, "How can I honor God (or my higher power) through my business today?" The answer might surprise you and lead you into fresh opportunities.

I want to encourage you to try at least one new practice from this chapter in your business this week. Maybe you hold a short team meeting to talk about your shared values. Or perhaps you set aside time each morning to pray over your to-do list. Whatever step you choose, do it with a hopeful heart. Believe that when you blend faith and work, you tap into a powerful source of creativity, wisdom, and love.

In the end, spiritual entrepreneurship is about living fully and serving joyfully. It is about letting your faith shape the way you earn a living, so your business becomes a channel of good in the world. You have everything you need to begin. Now, take that next step forward, trusting that each step of faith will light the path for you and for everyone your business touches.

PART II

BUILDING FAITH-FUELED HABITS

03

DAILY DISCIPLINE AND DEVOTION

*"But seek first the kingdom of God and His righteousness,
and all these things shall be added to you."*

(MATTHEW 6:33)

Setting the Tone for Your Day

Imagine you wake up each morning feeling calm and steady, ready to face whatever comes your way. You have a quiet confidence that no matter how busy or challenging the day gets, you can stay on track. This sense of peace and readiness comes from having a daily discipline and devotion practice. When you take a little time each day to focus on your spirit and your goals, you set a strong tone for everything else.

A routine of daily discipline and devotion helps you grow in faith, sharpen your mind, and build healthy habits. It can be as simple as a few minutes of prayer or quiet time, followed by writing down your most important tasks. Or it can be more detailed, with reading, journaling, exercise, or listening to uplifting music. The key is to find a pattern that works for you and stick to it. Over time, these small daily acts can bring big changes to your business and your life.

In this chapter, you will learn practical ways to create a morning routine (or an evening routine, if that fits you better). You will see how daily discipline and devotion link closely with your faith, giving you extra strength when you feel tired or overwhelmed. You will also read stories from my own journey, times when discipline helped me push through tough moments. By the end, you will be able to build a simple daily plan that keeps you focused on your business goals and your spiritual growth.

Why Daily Discipline Matters

Running a business can feel like juggling many balls at once. You have orders to fulfill, customers to please, and problems to solve. Without a steady routine, it is easy to get lost in the chaos. Your mind races from one task to another, and you start each day feeling stressed before you even begin.

Daily discipline is like creating a clear road for your day. You decide in advance what is most important and how you will spend your time. This gives you a sense of control. It tells your brain, "I know where I'm going and how to get there." With a plan in place, you can focus on tasks that matter instead of running in circles.

But discipline is not just about getting things done. It also shapes your character. You learn to keep promises to yourself. You train your mind to be steady, even when life feels shaky. Each time you follow through on a commitment—like spending quiet time in prayer or reading a chapter of a helpful book—you build your confidence. You show yourself and others that you can be trusted to do what you say.

For me, discipline became a lifeline when my schedule grew too crowded. I found that when I woke up early to pray, read something inspiring, and plan my day, I felt calmer. I noticed I made smarter decisions, and my work flowed more smoothly. On days I skipped my routine, I often felt scattered and overwhelmed. That contrast showed me how powerful daily discipline can be.

Devotion as Your Spiritual Anchor

Along with discipline, devotion is a key part of staying strong in faith. Devotion is the time you set aside to connect with God (or your higher power) each day. This could include prayer, reading scripture, meditating on a sacred text, or simply sitting quietly and listening for guidance.

Why does devotion matter so much? Because it feeds your soul. Just like your body needs regular meals, your spirit needs regular nourishment. In the rush of business, it is easy to forget that you are more than a worker or a boss. You are a person with hopes, fears, and dreams. Spending daily time in devotion reminds you that you are loved and guided by a power greater than yourself.

Devotion also helps you see your business in the bigger picture of life. You might start your day worried about an important meeting or a dip in sales. But when you step into a quiet moment of prayer, you remember that God is with you. You remember that your business is not just about money—it is also about serving people and growing in your calling. This perspective can calm your worries and fill you with a sense of purpose.

In my own life, I have felt the difference devotion makes. When I was launching my first major project, I woke up each day feeling nervous. Thoughts like "What if I fail?" ran through my mind. But by sitting in prayer for a few minutes each morning, I found peace. I would say, "God, please guide my steps. Please give me wisdom and courage." Soon, my heart would feel lighter, and I could move forward with faith.

Crafting a Morning Routine

A well-structured morning routine sets the tone for the whole day. You do not have to wake up at the crack of dawn, but choosing a time that gives you a little space before work starts can make a huge difference.

Here is a simple outline you can adjust to your needs:

Quiet Time or Prayer (5–15 minutes):

Begin your day by focusing on your spiritual side. If you pray, thank God for the new day and ask for guidance. If you meditate, do a few minutes of deep breathing. Let your thoughts settle.

Read Something Uplifting (5–10 minutes):

Find a short devotional, an encouraging article, or an inspiring quote. Read slowly and let the words sink in. If you have more time, you could study a passage of scripture or a chapter from a faith-based or motivational book.

Write Down Gratitudes (2–5 minutes):

List a few things you are thankful for—big or small. This habit trains your mind to look for blessings. It could be as simple as "clean water" or "a supportive friend." Gratitude refuels your spirit with positivity.

Review Your Goals (3–5 minutes):

Take a quick look at your short-term goals, like what you want to accomplish this week, and your long-term business vision. Remind yourself of your "Why," the purpose behind your business.

Plan Your Key Tasks (5–10 minutes):

Write down the top 3 things you must do today. These tasks should align with your goals. If you have extra time, you can list smaller tasks as well. But focus first on what truly moves the needle for your business and your calling.

This routine can be as short as 20 minutes or as long as an hour, depending on your situation. If you have kids, you might need to wake up earlier to find quiet time. If you have a flexible schedule, you could expand some parts, like reading or journaling. The goal is not perfection but consistency. Doing a short routine daily is better than doing a long routine only once in a while.

Designing an Evening Routine

While mornings set the day's tone, evenings can help you wind down and prepare for restful sleep. Having an evening routine prevents your mind from racing with unended tasks. It also lets you reflect on your day with gratitude and gather lessons learned.

Consider these steps for a peaceful evening routine:

Turn Off Screens Early:

Bright lights and social media scrolling can keep your mind too active. Try to switch off phones, tablets, or computers at least 30 minutes before bed. This helps your brain settle into a calmer state.

Journal or Reflect (5–10 minutes):

Write about your day. What went well? What challenges did you face? How did you handle them? Jot down any prayers or thoughts of gratitude. This reflection can help you see your progress and keep track of answers to prayer.

Plan Tomorrow's Top Tasks (3–5 minutes):

Quickly choose which tasks deserve your main focus tomorrow. This way, you will not lie awake worrying about what you need to do next. It also gives your mind a head start on problem-solving overnight.

Quiet Devotion or Prayer (5–10 minutes):

End your day by turning your heart back to God. Thank Him for the blessings you noticed. Ask for help with any worries. If you prefer silence, just breathe deeply and rest in the awareness that you are cared for.

Bedtime Reading (Optional):

If you like, read a chapter of an uplifting book or a short spiritual passage. This can ease you into sleep with peaceful thoughts. Stay away from negative news or information that may interrupt your sleep and thoughts.

Having an evening routine not only improves your rest but also strengthens your self-discipline. By ending your day with intention, you remind yourself that each moment—from sunrise to bedtime—is a gift that you can steward wisely.

Sticking to Your Routines

Starting a routine can feel exciting at first. You may look forward to having a calm morning or a peaceful evening. But as days pass, life can interfere. You might oversleep, deal with sudden problems, or simply feel unmotivated. So how do you stick to your routines?

Start Small

Do not try to cram too many tasks into your routine right away. Pick one or two steps to focus on, such as a short prayer time and a quick to-do list. Once you master those, you can add more.

Set Alarms or Reminders

Use your phone's alarm or calendar reminders to gently nudge you at key times. For example, set an alarm that says, "Morning Devotion" or "Evening Reflection." Over time, your body and mind will adjust.

Create a Cozy Space

If you have a comfortable chair or a specific corner of your home that feels peaceful, use it for your daily routines. Having a dedicated spot can help your brain recognize it is time to focus or wind down.

Ask for Accountability

Share your routine goals with a friend or family member. Check in with each other daily or weekly. A simple text like, "Did you do your morning prayer time today?" can be a big help.

Celebrate Progress

At the end of each week, notice how well you stuck to your routine. Celebrate small wins, like "I did my devotional four mornings this week." If you slipped up, do not be harsh. Reflect on what happened and adjust as needed.

When I first tried to wake up earlier for devotion, I set my alarm for a much earlier time than usual. I quickly failed because my body was not used to it. Then I made a smaller change—waking just 15 minutes earlier than before. That felt doable, and after a couple of weeks, I added another 15 minutes. By taking gradual steps, I built a habit that lasted.

Overcoming Challenges and Distractions

Even with the best plan, distractions will appear. Your phone might buzz with notifications. A neighbor might knock on your door for a chat. Or your own thoughts might wander to the tasks ahead. Overcoming these challenges takes awareness and gentle discipline.

Dealing with Digital Noise

Social media, news feeds, and emails can rob you of focus. During your devotion or planning time, consider putting your phone in another room or using "Do Not Disturb" mode. If you rely on your phone for an alarm, turn off unnecessary notifications. You want this time to be sacred, free from the "ping" of the outside world.

Handling Family or Roommate Interruptions

If you live with others, let them know you have a special routine. Ask for their support, explaining that this time helps you stay balanced and productive. Maybe you hang a small sign on your door that says, "Quiet Time." Or you pick a place in your home where you are not easily found—like a back porch or a quiet corner of the living room.

Taming Your Wandering Mind

Sometimes the biggest distraction is your own thoughts. You might sit down to pray and immediately start thinking about a problem at work. When this happens, simply notice it. Acknowledge the thought and gently guide your focus back to your prayer or reading. Over time, your mind becomes better trained to stay present.

Making Peace with Imperfection

Remember that no routine is perfect. Some days, life will throw surprises at you—like a sick child or an unexpected phone call. If you skip or shorten your routine once in a while, that is okay. Just return to it the next day. Consistency over the long run matters more than perfection in the short term.

I recall a hectic season when I was launching a new product. My phone seemed to ring nonstop with questions from team members and suppliers. To keep my morning devotion time safe, I started putting my phone on airplane mode. At first, I worried I would miss something urgent. But I found that 15 or 20 minutes of quiet focus was well worth it. When I turned the phone back on, I handled tasks more calmly because I felt grounded in my spirit.

Combining Discipline with Flexibility

You might wonder, "How can I be disciplined yet also stay open to God's leading?" The answer lies in balancing structure with flexibility. It is helpful to plan your day, but it is also wise to remain open if God sends unexpected opportunities or changes your direction.

Embrace a "Flexible Framework"

Think of your routine as a sturdy framework that you can adjust as needed. For instance, if your family decides to go out of town, you might shift your prayer time to the evening or find a quiet moment before bed in a hotel room. You do not abandon your practice, you simply adapt it to the new setting.

Listen for the Spirit's Promptings

Sometimes, you might feel led to extend your prayer time or do extra reading if you sense God is speaking to your heart. Other times, you might feel a nudge to visit someone who needs help, even if that is not on your plan. Trust these promptings. God often works in our lives through small, unexpected signals.

Review and Revise

Every month or two, take a look at your daily routine. Ask, "Is this still working for me?" Maybe you need to add more journaling or cut back on news reading. Being disciplined does not mean you are locked into the same routine forever. It means you intentionally shape your habits for your current season of life.

In my experience, God has gently rerouted my day at times. I remember a morning when I felt an unshakable urge to call a friend, even though I was in the middle of my usual routine. That friend was going through a personal crisis and really needed to hear a caring voice. If I had been too strict about my plan, I might have missed that divine assignment. Instead, I paused my reading, made the call, and trusted I could return to my routine later.

Building Physical Health into Discipline and Devotion

Your spiritual life and business success are also connected to your physical well-being. A tired or weak body can lower your energy and mood, making it harder to pray, think clearly, or handle stress. That is why a healthy lifestyle is part of daily discipline and devotion.

Simple Exercise

You do not need an intense workout routine to stay healthy. Even a short walk, some light stretches, or a 10-minute workout video can boost your energy. If you prefer the morning, you can exercise right after prayer. If evenings feel better, you can do it before bed. The main goal is to get your body moving.

Healthy Eating Habits

Choose foods that nourish you. Try to include fruits, vegetables, whole grains, and lean proteins in your meals. Limit sugary snacks and drinks that cause energy crashes. Drink plenty of water to stay hydrated. Treat your body like the precious temple it is.

Mindful Breaks

Throughout the day, schedule short breaks to stand up, breathe, or refocus. These mini-pauses can prevent burnout. They also give you a chance to reconnect with God. A quick prayer like, "Lord, guide me through the next hour," can bring peace amid a busy schedule.

Sleep Discipline

Getting enough rest is crucial. Aim for a regular bedtime that allows you 7–8 hours of sleep. If you struggle to fall asleep, avoid caffeine in the late afternoon or consider a calming bedtime ritual, like reading or listening to soft music.

I once neglected my health while pushing through a busy season. I ate fast food, stayed up too late, and skipped exercise. I told myself I was too busy for anything else. But soon, I felt drained and even a bit cranky. My morning devotion times felt dull because I was half asleep. Eventually, I realized that caring for my body was not selfish—it was necessary to show up fully for my work and my spiritual practices. So I began adding a short walk and healthier meals. My energy returned, and my prayer time became richer.

Using Tools and Technology Wisely

Technology can be a double-edged sword. It can distract you or help you stay on track, depending on how you use it. Here are a few ways to make technology your friend in daily discipline and devotion:

Calendar and To-Do Apps

Digital calendars like Google Calendar or apps like Todoist can help you plan your tasks. Set reminders for prayer times or reading. Color-code your calendar to distinguish between spiritual practices, work tasks, and personal time.

Faith-Based Apps

Some apps provide daily devotionals, Bible readings, or prayer prompts. If you like guided meditations or devotions, you can find plenty of options online. However, be sure to avoid the trap of surfing other apps during that time.

Focus Tools

Apps like "Focus@Will" or website blockers can help you avoid social media or news sites during your devotion or work sessions. These tools keep your mind from wandering.

Digital Notes and Journaling

If you prefer typing over handwriting, apps like Evernote or OneNote let you keep a digital journal. You can also store quotes or reflections that inspire you.

Listening Resources

Podcasts and audiobooks on faith or entrepreneurship can be part of your routine. You could listen while you exercise or cook breakfast. Just be sure to include some quiet time, too. Constant noise—even good noise—can crowd out your own inner voice.

I use a simple note-taking app to record my prayers and insights. I like that I can search for key words later and see how God answered certain prayers. It also helps me spot patterns—like if I am worrying about the same issue over and over. This digital journal has become a valuable part of my daily devotion.

Stories of Discipline and Devotion in Action

To show how daily discipline and devotion can transform lives, let me share two short stories:

The Early-Bird Entrepreneur

A friend of mine named Sarah runs an online clothing boutique. She used to roll out of bed, grab her phone, and immediately dive into emails. She felt stressed and anxious before she even brushed her teeth. Then she learned about creating a morning devotion. She started waking up 30 minutes earlier to pray, read a short Bible passage, and jot down her main tasks for the day. Over time, she noticed she was calmer and more focused. Her business decisions improved, and her relationship with customers thrived because she was not operating from a place of panic.

The Overworked Father

Another friend, Michael, struggled to balance his job with family responsibilities. He felt distant from God and short-tempered with his kids. He decided to end each day with a simple evening routine— just 10 minutes of journaling what went well that day and a short prayer of gratitude. Sometimes, his kids joined in, sharing what they were thankful for. This new habit helped Michael sleep better, feel closer to his faith, and reconnect with his family. He said it was like "turning off the stress switch" each night.

These examples show that daily discipline and devotion do not have to be complicated to be effective. Even short, consistent practices can bring peace, joy, and clarity to your business and personal life.

Personal Testimony—My Breakthrough Moment

I want to share a personal breakthrough I had when I truly embraced daily discipline and devotion. There was a season when I was juggling multiple roles: expanding my business, mentoring new entrepreneurs, and volunteering at my church. I felt like I was always behind schedule. My prayer time became rushed or skipped. My to-do list was never-ending. I snapped at my family for small things. Deep inside, I felt guilty and disconnected.

One evening, I collapsed on my couch, totally drained. I opened my journal and wrote, "God, I cannot keep doing this. Please guide me." Right then, I felt a gentle nudge to regain control of my mornings. I realized I needed a structured, faith-centered routine. So I made a plan:

- Wake up at 5:30 a.m.
- Pray and read a short devotional for 15 minutes.
- Spend 10 minutes journaling what I was thankful for and writing down my top 3 tasks.
- Eat a healthy breakfast.

The first week was tough. I wanted to hit snooze. I felt restless during prayer because my mind wandered. But I stuck with it. Slowly, I noticed a shift. I felt more peaceful. My tasks became clearer, and I was less stressed about juggling everything. My family noticed I was kinder, more patient. My team saw I was more focused and present during meetings.

A month later, I realized I had gone from feeling burned out to feeling energized. That morning routine was my lifeline. It reminded me daily that my strength came from God, not from my own frantic efforts. It also helped me make better business decisions. Instead of chasing every opportunity, I chose projects that aligned with my values. My business actually performed better, even though I was working fewer hours, because the hours I did work were filled with clear purpose.

Looking back, I see that daily discipline and devotion changed not only my schedule, but also my heart. It turned my frantic striving into a steady rhythm. I still have busy seasons, but I know how to anchor myself: return to my morning plan, slow down, and trust that God will guide me step by step.

Your Path to Steadiness and Growth

A daily discipline and devotion practice might seem like a small thing, but it has the power to create big changes in your life and business. It keeps you centered in faith, helps you manage your time, and shapes you into a leader who can handle stress with grace. By setting aside even a short window each day for prayer, reading, reflection, and planning, you build strong spiritual and mental muscles.

Remember, there is no single "right" way to do this. Each person's routine will look different based on their schedule, personality, and stage of life. The important thing is to be consistent and genuine. When you meet with God each day—whether in the morning or at night— you open yourself to wisdom and peace that goes beyond your own understanding.

Over time, these daily habits will ripple through every part of your life. You will notice you have more patience with family and co-workers. You will tackle business challenges with a calm focus instead of panic. You will feel supported by a greater power who cares about your success and well-being. And when setbacks happen—as they always do—you will have a steady anchor to keep you from drifting.

Now is the perfect time to start. Whether you create a full morning routine or begin with just five minutes of quiet time, take that first step. Ask God to bless your efforts, and trust that each small act of discipline will pave the way for greater growth. By committing to daily discipline and devotion, you are investing in your own strength, your business's future, and your deeper walk of faith.

This is your journey, and it unfolds one day at a time. May you find joy in each step, comfort in your daily devotion, and unshakable faith as you build the life and business you are called to create.

04

MINDSET MASTERY

"Do not be conformed to this world, but be transformed by the renewal of your mind..."

(ROMANS 12:2)

Your Mind, Your Greatest Ally

Picture yourself standing at the start of a long road. You see hills, valleys, and curves in the distance. You feel both excited and a little afraid. How you view that road—and your chances of getting to the end—will shape your whole journey. This is how mindset works in your business and in life. When you believe you can keep going, you are more likely to overcome obstacles. When you see problems as chances to learn, you grow stronger. And when you choose faith over fear, you open yourself to wonderful possibilities.

Your mindset is like the captain steering a ship. It gives instructions to every part of your life. If the captain's directions are hopeful and wise, the ship sails smoothly. But if the captain is filled with doubt, the ship wanders off course or even sinks. In business, your mindset can push you to try bold ideas, or it can hold you back with worry. It can help you face tough competitors, or it can leave you stuck in fear.

This chapter is about mastering your mindset so that it becomes your greatest ally instead of your worst enemy. You will learn simple steps to build a positive mental outlook, break free from doubt, and handle challenges with courage. You will see how faith can guide your thoughts, keeping them steady even when life feels stormy. As you apply these lessons, you will find yourself seeing problems as puzzles you can solve, failures as temporary setbacks, and each day as a fresh chance to grow.

I remember a time when my own mindset felt fragile. I had launched a new product, but sales were slow. Doubts started to whisper, "You are not good enough. This will never work." My stomach was in knots, and I lost sleep worrying about bills. Then, I realized something important: my thinking was as much of a problem as any business hurdle. By shifting my mindset—leaning on faith and focusing on solutions—things began to change. I found fresh ideas and the courage to keep going. That is the power of mindset mastery.

The Power of Positive Thoughts

Your thoughts shape the world around you, even if you do not realize it. When you fill your mind with fear, you start looking for reasons to give up. You might notice only the barriers and ignore the helpers or open doors around you. On the other hand, when you fill your mind with hope, you become more alert to possibilities. You see tiny clues that lead to new ideas. You spot people who might lend a hand.

Positive thinking does not mean you pretend problems do not exist. It means you trust there is always a way forward, even if you have to search hard for it. You look at roadblocks and say, "I can find a way around this." When you make a mistake, you tell yourself, "This is a lesson I can learn from," rather than, "I am a failure."

Did you know that the thoughts you dwell on eventually come out in your words and actions? Imagine you start your day by saying, "I am so tired. Everything will go wrong." You carry that mood into every call and meeting. People pick up on your gloom, and suddenly, you have a harder time connecting with customers or solving problems. But if you start your day with, "I am thankful for a new morning. I am ready for good things," you walk into your tasks with energy. That energy sparks better ideas, stronger solutions, and warmer connections.

Faith ties into this because when you trust in a higher power, you have a baseline of hope. You believe that no matter how tough life gets, you are not alone. You know that help can appear from unexpected places. This belief brightens your thoughts and encourages you to remain positive. Over time, you see more blessings unfold, and your faith grows even stronger.

Understanding Your Inner Critic

Inside each person's mind is a small voice that can be harsh or critical—this is your "inner critic." That voice says things like, "You are not smart enough," or "You are going to fail." Sometimes, it even sounds like the voice of a parent, teacher, or bully from your past. Other times, it is your own fear in disguise, trying to protect you from embarrassment or pain.

Your inner critic might become louder when you step outside your comfort zone. Maybe you are trying a new marketing approach or pitching a big client. Right before you act, you hear, "They will never like your idea" or "You are wasting your time." This can cause you to freeze up or back away from opportunities. You might even talk yourself out of trying at all.

Here is the key: your inner critic is not always telling the truth. In fact, it often twists facts and jumps to negative conclusions. By becoming aware of this voice, you can question it. Instead of instantly believing those discouraging thoughts, you can ask, "Is that really true? Where is the evidence?"

One thing I do when I sense my inner critic flaring up is to write down the negative thought in a journal. Then, I list reasons that thought might be false. For example, if my mind says, "No one will buy your new service," I remind myself of people who have already shown interest or left good feedback. Just seeing facts on paper can calm the fear. It is like shining a light on a shadowy corner.

Your inner critic might never fully go away. However, you can learn to recognize its voice and refuse to give it full control. Over time, its power weakens because you stop giving its words so much weight. You replace those false statements with truthful, encouraging ones. This is an important step in mastering your mindset.

Breaking Free from Limiting Beliefs

A limiting belief is a belief that holds you back from reaching your full potential. You might say, "I am terrible at public speaking," or "I am too old to start a business." These beliefs can grow so strong that they shape your actions. You avoid speaking events or never pursue your dream venture. In reality, these are just stories you tell yourself.

Where do limiting beliefs come from? Sometimes, they start with a negative experience—like failing a test and thinking you are "dumb." Other times, they grow from cultural messages or comments made by others, like "Girls are not good at math," or "Artists cannot make a living." Over time, you accept these ideas as truth, and they form mental walls around your future.

To break free, you can do a belief "inventory." Write down some of your core beliefs about yourself, your abilities, and your future. Then, examine them one by one. Ask, "Is this always true? Is there a time I proved this belief wrong?" You might be surprised at how many of your negative ideas are not facts, but old stories that no longer fit who you are.

Next, replace the limiting belief with a more empowering statement. For example, "I am bad at public speaking" becomes "I am improving at public speaking, and I can learn the skills I need." This is not just empty cheerleading—it is a reminder that you can grow. God has given you a mind that learns and a spirit that can persevere. Faith teaches that you are capable of growth, and science agrees that the human brain can develop new skills with practice.

Over time, consistently challenging your limiting beliefs will transform your mindset. You will feel braver about trying new things and more willing to accept both success and failure as part of the journey. You will also discover that many "walls" you thought were concrete were actually illusions you could pass through by changing your thoughts.

Reprogramming Your Mind for Success

Your mind is like a computer—it runs on programs built from your experiences, habits, and beliefs. If these programs are negative or outdated, they slow you down. Fortunately, you can rewrite them. This process is called reprogramming your mind.

Affirmations:

An affirmation is a positive statement about yourself or your future, spoken as though it is already true. For instance, you might say, "I am confident and prepared to handle any challenge." When you repeat affirmations daily, you create new thought patterns that replace harmful self-talk.

Visualization:

Visualization means imagining yourself succeeding in vivid detail. For example, if you want to open a bakery, close your eyes and picture the shop in the morning sunlight. See the smiling customers, smell the fresh bread, and feel the joy of providing delicious treats. This mental rehearsal trains your brain to believe this future is possible.

Gratitude Practice:

By focusing on what you already have, you tell your mind, "I am blessed, and I expect more good things." Every day, list at least three things you are grateful for. This can be simple, like a roof over your head or a friend who supports you. Gratitude helps break scarcity thinking—where you believe there is not enough to go around—and replaces it with abundance thinking.

Self-Compassion:

Treat yourself as you would a dear friend. When you make a mistake, do not lash out internally. Say, "It is okay, I am learning," or "I can do better next time." This gentle approach helps you bounce back from errors rather than getting stuck in shame.

Reflection and Prayer:

Faith-based entrepreneurs can use prayer to ask for help in reprogramming the mind. You might say, "God, please renew my mind. Help me release these old, harmful beliefs." Reflection in a journal can also help you spot patterns, like a recurring fear or a repeated limiting statement.

Reprogramming your mind takes time, just like learning a new language. You have spent years with certain beliefs, so do not expect them to vanish overnight. But with patience and daily practice, you will see shifts. You will start catching negative thoughts faster and replacing them with thoughts that empower you. Bit by bit, you craft a mindset built for success.

Using Faith to Strengthen Your Mindset

Faith and mindset are close partners. Faith reminds you that your life has purpose and that you are supported by a power greater than yourself. This belief can soothe fears, reduce stress, and give you a reason to keep going when results are slow. Many people pray for strength, guidance, and wisdom in their business decisions. This practice can calm the mind and open new insights.

When you believe God (or your higher power) cares about you, it is easier to trust the process. You do not feel as rushed to force outcomes or panic when doors close. You might pray, "If this opportunity is not right for me, please guide me to a better one." This kind of surrender helps you avoid mental burnout. It also frees up mental space to solve problems creatively.

Scripture or spiritual teachings often have principles that support a healthy mindset. For example, teachings about courage, perseverance, and love can shape how you view competition, failure, or tough customers. Instead of lashing out, you practice patience. Instead of giving up, you practice endurance. Over time, these spiritual truths become the backbone of your mindset.

I recall a time when I lost a key client unexpectedly. Financially, it stung. Mentally, I felt a wave of panic. Yet through prayer and journaling, I sensed a gentle voice saying, "I have something better ahead. Trust Me." I chose to believe that message. A few weeks later, I landed an even bigger client who was a perfect match. This taught me that faith-based trust can ease the blow of disappointments and keep your mind clear for new blessings.

Daily Mindset Exercises

Just like lifting weights builds strong muscles, daily mindset exercises can strengthen your inner world. Here are a few practices you can weave into your morning or evening routine:

Morning Check-In:

Right when you wake up, pause and ask yourself, "How am I feeling? What thoughts are on my mind?" Notice if they are mostly negative or positive. Then, set a simple intention, like "Today, I choose to focus on gratitude." This small step alerts your brain to watch for blessings.

Midday Affirmation Break:

Halfway through your day, take a minute to speak an affirmation. It could be, "I am creative. I find solutions easily." You might keep a sticky note on your desk or a reminder on your phone. This interrupts any stress spiral and re-centers your mind on possibility.

End-of-Day Reflection:

Before bed, think about one situation that challenged you. Ask, "What did I learn? What did I do well?" Even if the day had some disappointments, spotting a silver lining teaches your brain that each event holds lessons. Over time, you become more resilient.

Mindful Breathing:

When your mind races with worry, close your eyes and take three slow, deep breaths. Inhale through your nose, hold for a second, then exhale through your mouth. As you breathe, imagine tension leaving your body. This technique calms the nervous system and helps you refocus.

Faith Anchors:

If you have a favorite scripture, devotion, or quote, read it several times a day. Let it sink into your heart. Say a short prayer asking for guidance. These faith anchors keep you connected to hope, reminding you that you are never alone.

These exercises do not have to be long. Even two minutes of mindfulness can refresh your mindset. The goal is consistency—doing them regularly enough that they become a natural part of your routine. Over time, your default thinking shifts to be more optimistic, calm, and open to growth.

Overcoming Self-Doubt

Self-doubt is the worry that you are not able to accomplish your dreams. It can creep in when you are faced with a new challenge or a big goal. Maybe you feel excited to write a book or launch a product, but then that tiny voice says, "Who do you think you are? You will never succeed."

The first step in overcoming self-doubt is recognizing that many successful people feel it, too. It is not a sign that you are destined to fail. It is simply your mind trying to protect you from the pain of failure. Yet, when you listen to that fear too much, you miss out on growth and joy.

Next, break your big goal into smaller tasks. If you want to open a store, start by making a list of what you need: a location, a business plan, some financing, and so on. Tackle one item at a time. Each little win, like securing a small loan or finding a potential storefront, proves to your mind that you can do this.

Also, lean on faith to remind you of your worth. You are more than a business owner or a job title. You are a creation with unique gifts. Reading encouraging scriptures or praying for confidence can lift your spirit. Sometimes, I recite a short prayer: "Lord, I feel uncertain. Please give me strength and remind me I am capable in Your eyes." This does not mean I avoid hard work. It means I trust that as I do my part, God does His part in guiding me.

If your self-doubt gets too heavy, talk to a mentor or a close friend. Honest conversation can break the power of hidden fears. You might find they have faced similar doubts. Hearing someone else's story can help you see that self-doubt is normal, but it does not have the final say.

Building a Support System

No one achieves mindset mastery alone. You need people who believe in you, offer fresh ideas, and remind you of your talents when you forget. A support system can include friends, family, mentors, fellow entrepreneurs, or faith groups.

Friends and Family:

Choose the ones who speak life into your dreams, not the ones who tear you down. Surrounding yourself with negative voices will drain your energy. Seek out those who say, "I'm proud of you," or "I know you can do it."

Mentors:

A mentor is someone who has walked the path you want to travel. They can share tips and warn you about common pitfalls. Listening to their stories and advice helps you see what is possible. A mentor also holds you accountable, checking in on your progress and mindset.

Fellow Entrepreneurs:

Join a group—online or in person—where people share business tips and encourage one another. When you see others pushing through challenges, it motivates you to do the same. You learn from their successes and from their mistakes.

Faith Community:

A church group, prayer group, or spiritual gathering can offer a safe space to share fears and wins. You can pray for each other and celebrate breakthroughs. In tough moments, knowing others are lifting you up in prayer can be a comfort unlike any other.

When I started my consulting business, I found a small circle of like-minded people at my church. We met once a week to pray for each other's ventures. We swapped resources and offered feedback on each other's ideas. Some of them had faced bigger challenges than I ever had. Seeing how they leaned on God and stayed positive inspired me. My mindset improved, and I learned that community is a gift from above.

A Personal Testimony—My Mindset Shift

I want to share a personal story about a time my mindset almost cost me a big opportunity. A few years ago, I was invited to speak at a local business conference. Initially, I was thrilled. But as the event drew closer, worry crept in: "What if I forget my words on stage? What if no one cares about my topic?"

My negative thoughts spiraled. I almost told the organizer I could not do it. Then, a mentor reminded me, "This is a chance to share your gifts. Don't let fear steal it away." I prayed, "God, please help me see this opportunity with hope instead of fear." I wrote affirmations like, "I am prepared. I speak clearly and confidently."

On the day of the talk, my heart raced, but I pushed through. I focused on serving the audience, not my fears. And guess what? My speech went well. People came up afterward, thanking me for the insights. A few even asked if I could coach them. This confirmed that my old doubts were just that—doubts, not facts.

That experience taught me a powerful lesson: mindset can either block you from sharing your gifts or open the door to new heights. By shifting from fear to faith, I stepped into a blessing I almost rejected. Now, whenever a new challenge arises, I remember that day. I remind myself that if I overcame worry then, I can overcome it again.

Mindset in the Face of Failure

Failure is a natural part of trying new things. Even the most successful people have stumbled. The difference is not in how many times they fail, but in how they respond to failure. Your mindset determines whether you see a failed attempt as a dead end or as a stepping stone.

A growth mindset says, "I can learn from this. Let me see what went wrong and fix it next time." A fixed mindset says, "I must be terrible. I will never try that again." Which one you choose will shape your future. If you pick the growth mindset, you keep moving. If you pick the fixed mindset, you get stuck.

Faith can help you see failure differently. You might pray, "God, show me what I can learn from this setback." Instead of sinking into shame or anger, you open yourself to wisdom. Sometimes, a closed door leads you to a better path. Other times, you just need to improve your approach before trying again. Either way, you trust that failure is not the final chapter.

I recall launching a product that got almost zero sales. It stung. My first reaction was to think, "I'm no good at marketing." But after some prayer and honest talks with mentors, I realized I had not studied my target audience closely. The product solved a problem few people had. So I pivoted. I tweaked the product to address a more common need and tried again. Sales improved. That failure became a valuable teacher, one I would have missed if I let shame shut me down.

Leading Others with a Strong Mindset

If you have a team or work with partners, your mindset affects them, too. People look to you for guidance. They notice how you react to stress or setbacks. If you stay calm and forward-thinking, they follow your lead. If you panic and speak words of doom, they feel alarmed and lose focus.

Leading with a strong mindset means being real about challenges, but also keeping faith in a positive outcome. You might say, "Yes, this problem is serious. But here is how we can tackle it. I believe we can find a solution." You model resilience by showing that mistakes are fixable, and brainstorming is welcome.

Also, share mindset tools with your team. Encourage them to use affirmations, gratitude lists, or reflection times. If someone is stuck in negativity, speak life into them. Remind them of their past successes. Show them how to reframe a problem as a puzzle to solve. When the whole team adopts a growth mindset, you create a culture of possibility instead of a culture of dread.

My first time leading a small team, I noticed one member was always down on himself. He would say, "I'm just not creative." His mindset limited his contributions. I scheduled a 1-on-1 chat, praised the good work he had done, and suggested we practice quick brainstorming sessions without judging ideas. Over time, he learned to relax and share more. This shift not only helped him—it boosted the entire team's creativity.

Putting Mindset Mastery into Practice

You have learned about the power of positive thoughts, facing your inner critic, breaking limiting beliefs, and using faith to anchor your mind. Now, how do you make mindset mastery a daily reality?

1. Create a Mindset Checklist:

Write down a few key points you want to remember every morning. For example:

- I am capable of growth.
- I will focus on solutions, not problems.
- I trust God to guide me.
- Challenges are chances to learn.

Keep this list where you can see it—maybe on your desk or as your phone wallpaper.

2. Surround Yourself with Encouragement:

Fill your environment with uplifting quotes, scripture verses, or photos that spark joy. Remove items that trigger negativity, if possible. This includes limiting your exposure to overly negative news or social media.

3. Seek Positive Influences:

Listen to podcasts or read books that push you toward a growth mindset. Follow social media accounts that post inspiring content. The more you feed your mind with uplifting ideas, the easier it is to stay positive.

4. Set Growth-Oriented Goals:

Aim for goals that stretch you beyond your comfort zone. Celebrate each inch of progress. For example, if you fear public speaking, set a goal to give a short talk in a friendly setting, like a local community group. Each success builds your confidence.

5. Reflect with Gratitude:

End each day by writing down one mindset win. Maybe you caught a negative thought and flipped it around. Maybe you tried something new and did not let fear stop you. These small wins add up.

6. Pray for Inner Transformation:

Ask God to keep working on your heart and mind. Trust that you are being shaped into someone who can handle bigger responsibilities and blessings. Faith is a powerful tool for lasting change because it connects your mindset to a divine source of power.

Mindset mastery is a continuous journey. You will not be perfectly positive all the time. You will have days when doubt creeps in or you slip into old patterns. The goal is not perfection but progress. Each time you catch a negative belief and replace it with a healthier one, you grow stronger. Each time you press on despite fear, your faith muscles get bigger.

Transforming Your World from the Inside Out

Your mindset shapes the lens through which you see everything—your business, your relationships, and your own capabilities. When that lens is clear and hopeful, you find solutions, attract good opportunities, and recover from setbacks with grace. When that lens is cloudy with fear or doubt, you miss chances to grow and bless others.

By learning to master your thoughts, you open the door to greater success, fulfillment, and peace. You understand that failures are not the end, but steps in your journey. You discover that your mind can be trained, like a muscle, to default to hope instead of dread. You realize that with faith guiding you, there is always a reason to believe in better outcomes.

This is your moment to commit to a new way of thinking. You have the tools: positive affirmations, reflection, faith, and supportive people who want to see you thrive. Each day is an opportunity to practice these tools, noticing your progress as fear loosens its grip and belief takes its place. Whether your dream is to launch a startup, become a well-known artist, or lead a team toward a shared vision, it starts in your mind.

As you move forward, remember the deeper truth: you are more than your worries. You are more than your old failures. You have a calling, and your mindset can either carry you toward it or steer you away.

Choose to let your mind be a faithful companion, fueled by hope, grounded in faith, and open to miracles. Walk in confidence, trusting that each step of growth in your mindset is one step closer to the destiny waiting for you.

05
THE ART OF RESILIENT THINKING

"I can do all things through Christ who strengthens me."

(PHILIPPIANS 4:13)

Bending Without Breaking

Have you ever watched a tree in a strong windstorm? Its branches sway wildly, but the trunk stays rooted. Sometimes, a branch might snap, but the tree itself often remains standing. This ability to bend without breaking is called resilience. In your life and in your business, you will face sudden storms—like losing a big client, running out of funds, or getting difficult feedback. How do you stay upright when these challenges hit? The answer lies in something called resilient thinking.

Resilient thinking is the art of seeing possibility instead of despair. It is looking at a setback and saying, "I can learn from this," rather than, "I am doomed." It is trusting that God is with you, even when life feels uncertain. Instead of getting stuck in fear, you search for the next step forward. In this chapter, you will learn what resilient thinking is, why it matters, and how to make it part of your daily life.

You do not have to be born with a special gift to be resilient. Like any skill, it can be learned and sharpened. Resilient thinking is your mental shield when criticism comes your way. It is your anchor when the business plan falls apart. It is also your hope when you are not sure how the next bill will be paid. Through faith, practice, and an open mind, you can grow a resilience that amazes others—and sometimes, even yourself.

I remember my first major setback as a business owner. My best-paying client decided to work with someone else. It felt like the ground was slipping away under my feet. I had rent and bills coming up, and I wondered if I should shut down my business. But something in my heart said, "Keep going." Over time, I replaced my fear with small steps forward. I prayed, asked for help, took new risks. That moment taught me how resilience can turn a huge loss into a turning point for growth.

What Is Resilient Thinking?

Resilient thinking is a mindset that bounces back after facing challenges. Imagine a rubber ball. When you drop it, it hits the floor and then bounces up again. This is how resilient thinkers respond to problems. Yes, they still feel disappointment or worry, but they do not let those feelings glue them to the ground. Instead, they ask, "What can I do now?" or "How can I make the best of this?"

> *"Our greatest weakness lies in giving up. The most certain way to succeed is always to try just one more time."*

- THOMAS EDISON

At its core, resilient thinking goes beyond just being positive. It means facing reality while choosing hope. You might admit, "This situation is tough" or "I feel hurt." But you also say, "I will keep trying," or "There might be a lesson in this." Sometimes, you find new solutions you have never seen before.

One way to check if you have resilient thinking is to watch how you react to unexpected changes. Suppose your new product launch fails. Do you instantly say, "I am a big failure, and I should give up"? Or do you pause, look at what happened, and figure out a better way to reach your customers? Resilience does not mean ignoring the pain of a setback. It means not getting stuck in that pain.

Sometimes, people confuse resilience with toughness. They think, "I have to be tough and never show weakness." But real resilience allows you to acknowledge your feelings and then choose your next step with a clear mind. Faith plays a big role here because it reminds you that even if you feel weak, God can be your strength. You do not have to power through on your own.

I once met a small business owner who had to close his store due to sudden rent increases. He felt heartbroken. But instead of letting that moment end his dream, he went online and started selling the same products through a simple website. Before long, he reached more customers than ever. That is resilient thinking at work—turning a closed door into a new path.

Why Resilient Thinking Matters in Business

In any business, problems will come. Sales might slump. A key employee might quit. A product might get bad reviews. Without resilience, these events can feel like the end of the road. You might see no way out and quit too soon. But with resilient thinking, each challenge becomes a puzzle you can solve.

Resilience also helps you stay calm under stress. When everything feels chaotic, a steady mindset stands out. Your team, customers, or partners will look to you for guidance. If you handle problems with composure, they gain confidence. They think, "If you can remain hopeful, maybe things are not as bad as they seem." In this way, your resilience can calm others around you.

Moreover, resilient thinking makes you more creative. People who panic or lose hope often cannot see beyond the problem. Their mind is stuck on negative thoughts: "This is terrible. I am doomed." But when you trust that a solution exists, your mind stays open. You begin to brainstorm, ask for help, or try fresh ideas. This creativity often leads to breakthroughs you would never have found if you had given up right away.

Faith strengthens resilience by offering a bigger perspective. You realize that life is more than this single setback. You remember that God has been faithful before and can be faithful again. This hope can give you the energy to keep trying, even when the odds look poor. Sometimes, breakthroughs happen right at the moment you are about to quit.

I saw this play out when a friend's bakery faced sudden competition from a big chain. Sales dropped, and she worried she could not compete on price. But she decided not to throw in the towel. Instead, she focused on the personal touch and homemade feel that the big chain lacked. She offered unique flavors and started a weekly newsletter with stories behind her recipes. Over time, loyal customers brought in new ones, and her bakery survived. Without resilience, she might have closed her doors at the first sign of trouble.

The Role of Perspective in Resilience

One of the main ingredients in resilient thinking is perspective. Perspective is how you choose to look at a situation. Imagine you put on glasses with red lenses. Suddenly, the whole world looks red. If you switch to blue lenses, the same world looks blue. Your mind works the same way. If you wear "fear lenses," everything looks scary and hopeless. If you wear "hope lenses," you see chances for growth and learning everywhere.

How do you shift your perspective from fear to hope? One way is to look at evidence of your past successes. Maybe you overcame a similar problem before. Maybe you grew in skill and faith through a trial. Remind yourself that you have survived tough times already. This helps you see that you can handle this new challenge too.

Another way is to zoom out. Instead of getting stuck in the current storm, think about the bigger story of your life. Ask, "Will this problem matter five years from now?" If the answer is no, you might realize you are blowing the problem out of proportion. If the answer is yes, it means you have a big challenge worth fighting for. Either way, you gain a clearer view that goes beyond the heat of the moment.

Faith also changes perspective by reminding you that you do not walk alone. When you pray, "God, help me see this situation clearly," you open your heart to divine guidance. You may still not have all the answers, but you feel less alone. This sense of companionship can lighten the weight of worry.

I once experienced a shipping delay that could have ruined my product launch. At first, I panicked. I assumed my entire plan was doomed. But then, I took a breath and prayed for a calmer perspective. I remembered that I could still communicate with my customers, explain the delay, and even offer a small gift for their patience. Instead of seeing the delay as a final blow, I saw it as a chance to show extra care. Many customers appreciated that effort and stayed loyal. My perspective had shifted from defeat to possibility.

Faith as the Root of Resilience

For many people, faith acts as the foundation that keeps them standing when storms come. It reminds you that you have a purpose bigger than any single setback. Even if your business plan fails, your value as a person remains. Your dreams might take a different shape, but your calling to do good in the world does not disappear.

Faith also provides a source of comfort. When no one else seems to understand your stress, God does. You can share your fears in prayer, knowing you are heard. This emotional release can refresh your heart and mind. After praying, you might feel a nudge to call a friend, seek a mentor, or try a new idea. Often, these nudges guide you toward unexpected blessings.

Another benefit of faith is the promise of hope. You learn that suffering can produce endurance, and endurance can grow your character. Each obstacle you overcome adds to your testimony. You can encourage others who face similar challenges by sharing how faith carried you through. This cycle of receiving help from God and then helping others can give your setbacks a deeper meaning.

I remember a time when I had a serious illness that forced me to pause my work. I felt behind on everything. Income stopped, and I worried about losing clients. Yet through prayer, I felt a calm assurance: "You need this time to rest. I will take care of the rest." During my recovery, a close friend stepped in to handle some of my tasks. Surprisingly, I did not lose clients—some even showed more support. That lesson taught me that faith is not about avoiding hardship; it is about trusting God to make a way through it.

Turning Setbacks into Stepping Stones

Resilient thinkers do not just survive setbacks; they use them as stepping stones to reach new heights. When a plan fails, they ask, "What can I learn from this?" They gather the lessons and apply them to their next attempt. They see mistakes as valuable teachers rather than signs of permanent defeat.

One method to turn setbacks into stepping stones is to reflect on what went wrong. This does not mean beating yourself up. It is about calmly asking, "Where did we drop the ball?" or "What was missing?" or "Did I communicate poorly?" By pinpointing the issue, you can fix it for the future. For instance, if your big advertising campaign flopped, maybe you realize you aimed at the wrong audience. Next time, you can target people who are more likely to buy your product.

Another method is to remain flexible. Sometimes, the path you planned is blocked, but a side road might still lead you to success. Let us say you dream of opening a physical store, but the rent in your area is too high. Rather than giving up, you could start an online shop first. You gain experience and build a customer base, preparing for a physical location later. Being flexible keeps you from hitting a dead end.

Lastly, keep your vision in mind. A setback might force you to change how you approach your dream, but it does not have to kill the dream itself. Maybe your timeline shifts, or your methods change. Resilience says, "I can wait, adapt, or find another route, but I am not giving up on the overall goal."

A friend of mine tried to launch a catering service, but the location she chose had almost no foot traffic. She took a financial hit after signing a lease and barely got any clients. Instead of throwing in the towel, she pivoted to offering meal deliveries and private chef services in people's homes. Within a year, she had steady clients who preferred the convenience of her coming to them. That first setback actually guided her to a more profitable business model.

Daily Habits for Building Resilient Thinking

Resilience is not a one-time decision. It grows through daily habits, like exercise for your mind. Just as you keep your body healthy by eating good food and moving around, you keep your spirit strong by feeding it hope and discipline.

Morning Reflection or Prayer:

Start each day with a few minutes of quiet. You can pray, meditate, or read something that inspires you. This habit sets a hopeful tone for the day ahead. You remind yourself that no matter what happens, you can handle it with God's help.

Affirmations and Encouraging Words:

Write down short statements that lift your spirit. For example, "I can find a way through any challenge," or "Each setback is a lesson for my growth." Repeat these sentences out loud, especially when you feel doubt creeping in.

Gratitude Journal:

Spend five minutes each evening listing a few things you are thankful for—maybe a kind word from a coworker, a new insight, or simply the roof over your head. Gratitude shifts your focus from what is lacking to what you already have, fueling a more positive outlook.

Healthy Boundaries with Negative Influences:

Limit your time around people or media that constantly feed you worry or despair. You do not have to avoid all tough news, but set wise boundaries. Balance any negative input with positive content— uplifting podcasts, encouraging friends, or music that lifts your mood.

Learning Routine:

Pick up a book or watch a short lesson that teaches you new skills related to your field. Becoming better at what you do boosts confidence. The more equipped you feel, the less helpless you become when problems arise.

Physical Care:

Remember your mind and body are linked. Getting enough sleep, staying active, and eating healthy meals help you respond to stress more calmly. If you feel tired or run-down, it is much harder to stay resilient.

By weaving these habits into your everyday life, you create a foundation for resilient thinking. Over time, you will notice that challenges do not knock you down as easily. You will also be faster to bounce back when things go wrong. Think of it as training your mind to stay steady in any storm.

Overcoming Doubt and Fear

Doubt and fear are like heavy weights that drag you down. They whisper, "You cannot do this. You are not good enough. Everything will fall apart." If left unchecked, these thoughts can keep you from even trying. But resilient thinking recognizes that doubt and fear, while normal, do not have to dominate your life.

One method to handle fear is to name it. When you feel that tightness in your chest or that sinking feeling in your stomach, pause. Ask, "What exactly am I afraid of?" Maybe you fear losing money, looking foolish, or disappointing loved ones. By naming the fear, you take away some of its mystery. It becomes a clear issue you can address, rather than a vague cloud haunting you.

Next, challenge the fear by asking, "Is there real evidence that my fear will come true?" Often, your mind exaggerates the worst-case scenario. If you have no evidence for your worry, remind yourself that you are dealing with a guess, not a fact. If the fear is realistic—like running out of money—then focus on solutions. You might make a cost-cutting plan, seek a loan, or add new revenue streams. Action shrinks fear.

Lean on faith by inviting God into your fears. Say, "Lord, I feel afraid. Please give me courage and wisdom." The act of prayer can soothe your nerves and remind you that you are not alone in this battle. Scripture often includes stories of people who overcame great odds through faith, which can encourage your heart.

Lastly, celebrate small victories. Every time you do something that scares you—even in a small way—you are flexing your resilience muscle. If you fear public speaking, but you speak up in a meeting anyway, that is a win. By noticing these brave moments, you show yourself that fear does not have to dictate your choices.

Encouraging Others to Stay Resilient

Resilience is not just about your personal journey. When you learn how to bounce back, you can help others do the same. Encouraging a friend, coworker, or family member who feels discouraged can lift them out of despair and give them hope.

Listen with Compassion:

Sometimes, people need to vent about their struggles. By listening without judgment, you let them know they are not alone. Offer a gentle nod or a reassuring word like, "I hear you. That sounds really tough."

Share Your Story:

If you have gone through a similar challenge, share how you overcame it. Hearing about real-life examples can spark hope. It tells the other person, "If you made it through, maybe I can too."

Speak Life-Giving Words:

Avoid phrases like, "Just get over it," which can sound dismissive. Instead, say, "I believe in your strength," or "I see potential in you." Reminding them of their good qualities and successes can help them shift from despair to determination.

Offer Practical Help:

Sometimes, resilience requires a helping hand. If someone is overwhelmed with tasks, maybe you can assist them for an afternoon. If they need advice, you can connect them to someone who has the answers. Small acts of support build a community of resilience.

Pray for Them:

If the person is open to prayer, offer to pray with or for them. Ask God to give them fresh hope and a clear mind. Feeling the unity of prayer can remind them that solutions might be closer than they think.

Encouraging others also strengthens your own resilience. There is something powerful about lifting someone else's spirit. It reminds you that humans are built to support and comfort each other. And often, as you give hope, you receive hope. That is the beauty of living in faith-centered community.

A Personal Testimony—My Toughest Test

I want to share a personal story about the hardest test of resilience I have ever faced. A few years ago, I poured all my savings into a new business venture. I believed in my product and my plan. I spent months building a website, working with designers, and testing samples. But at the worst possible moment—right before launch—

my main supplier shut down due to financial troubles. Suddenly, all my materials were gone, and the money I had spent seemed wasted.

I felt crushed. My mind buzzed with questions: "How could I be so unlucky? Why did I not see this coming?" I was tempted to quit right there and then. I remember dropping to my knees and praying, "God, I do not know what to do. Please help me think clearly. Give me resilience."

Later that day, I called a mentor who reminded me of my strengths: planning, networking, and creativity. He said, "Use those skills to find another supplier fast. Do not give up on your dream because of one big hurdle." Encouraged, I searched online, called contacts, and read reviews of other suppliers across the country. Within a week, I found a supplier who could deliver similar materials at almost the same price.

Yes, the launch was delayed. I had to explain the setback to my early customers, and some of them dropped out. But I kept going. Eventually, I made new connections that actually improved my product. In the end, the business found a solid footing. That moment taught me that resilience is not about never feeling worry or disappointment. It is about what you do next. You can stay stuck or you can start moving again, trusting that God will light your path step by step.

Practical Tools for Resilient Thinking

Now that you understand the value of resilient thinking, let us explore some practical tools you can use every day. These techniques can help you stay calm, flexible, and hopeful, even when trouble arrives.

The "Stop-Breathe-Pray" Method:

When anxiety hits, pause. Take three slow, deep breaths. Then say a short prayer, like, "God, give me clarity and peace right now." This brief break can stop you from reacting in panic. You gain a moment to plan a thoughtful response.

Problem-Solving Questions:

When you face a challenge, ask:

- "What is one thing I can do right now to make this better?"
- "Who can I talk to who might have ideas?"
- "Is there a different way to see this?"
- By focusing on solutions, you signal your brain to look for answers instead of dwelling on fear.

Worst-Case/Best-Case Balancing:

Your mind often jumps to the worst possible outcome. To balance this, also imagine the best case. Then, consider the most likely scenario, which is often somewhere in the middle. This balanced view can ease extreme worry.

Check Your Self-Talk:

Pay attention to your inner dialogue. If you hear "I always mess up," replace it with "I am learning and improving." If you catch "I am hopeless," swap it for "I still have options." Over time, kinder self-talk becomes your new default.

Time for Fun and Rest:

Resilience does not mean working 24/7. It involves rest and joyful moments to recharge your mind and spirit. Schedule breaks, hobbies, or outings with friends. When you return to your tasks, you will have a fresher perspective.

Faith Journaling:

Keep a notebook where you track prayers, answers you see, and moments you feel God's guidance. Reading past entries can remind you how far you have come and how many tight spots you have escaped. It boosts your faith in future deliverance.

These tools may feel awkward at first, but with practice, they become part of your routine. In time, you will see that you handle stress better and bounce back faster. You will also find you have more energy to devote to growth instead of simply firefighting problems.

Leading with Resilience

As you develop resilient thinking, you can become a pillar of strength for others around you—your team, family, friends, or community. Leading with resilience means setting a tone of hope and courage. It means you do not hide challenges from your group, but you guide them in finding solutions.

Be Transparent (Yet Encouraging):

If your business hits a rough patch, do not pretend everything is perfect. Your team will sense something is off. Instead, share the truth in a calm way. Let them see you are aware of the problem but also confident there is a way forward.

Model Resilient Behavior:

People watch how you handle stress. If you get angry or blame others, they might copy that. If you remain calm, they learn to do the same. By practicing resilient thinking in front of them, you teach by example.

Foster a "Growth Mindset" Culture:

In your workplace or group, reward people who try new ideas, even if they fail sometimes. Talk openly about lessons learned from mistakes. This builds a team that is not afraid to take risks and innovate.

Empower Others with Faith:

If faith is part of your leadership style, do not be shy to encourage those who are open to it. A short prayer or a gentle reminder of God's care can calm anxious hearts. Of course, respect everyone's beliefs, but do not hide your own source of hope.

Celebrate Resilience Together:

When you overcome a challenge as a group, take time to celebrate. Thank those who put in extra effort. Reflect on what worked and how you want to handle future problems. Recognition boosts morale and cements resilient practices in your culture.

Leading with resilience does not mean you will never feel stress. It means you accept stress as part of the process and guide people through it with grace. Over time, your team becomes stronger, and your bond grows deeper. You also develop a reputation for handling challenges well, which can attract partnerships or customers who respect your steady approach.

Putting It All Together—Your Resilient Journey

You have explored many sides of resilient thinking—what it is, why it matters, and how faith supports it. You have learned daily habits that build resilience and tools to handle fear and doubt. You have seen how you can lead others by modeling this mindset. Now, it is time to put everything together in your own journey.

Identify Your Greatest Challenge:

Think about the biggest storm you are facing right now. It might be a failing product, a tough financial situation, or a conflict in your team. Write it down.

Apply Resilient Thinking:

Reflect on what you have learned in this chapter. Can you shift your perspective by recalling past successes? Can you pick a tool like "Stop-Breathe-Pray" to calm yourself? Are there practical steps or problem-solving questions to try?

Reach Out:

Resilience is not a solo act. Who can you talk to for advice or encouragement? It might be a mentor, a friend, or someone in your faith community. Asking for help is not weakness; it is wisdom.

Move Forward in Faith:

Make one small decision today that moves you closer to a solution. Maybe you schedule a meeting, revise a plan, or reach out to a new customer base. Before you take action, say a short prayer: "God, guide me and give me courage."

Celebrate Every Step:

Even if you only make a tiny improvement, recognize it. Building resilience is like climbing a mountain. Each step is progress, even if you cannot see the summit yet.

Remember, resilience is a journey you walk day by day. Some days, you will feel strong and confident. Other days, you might stumble. That is normal. True resilience is built through ups and downs, each challenge adding to your story of perseverance. As you trust God and apply these lessons, you will see a change in how you face obstacles. Your storms might not shrink, but your capacity to handle them will grow—and that is the essence of resilient thinking.

A Future of Strength and Hope

Resilient thinking empowers you to face life's storms without collapsing. It turns obstacles into opportunities for growth. It reminds you that failure is not the end, just a chapter in your bigger story. Rooted in faith, it gives you the courage to move forward even when you cannot see the entire path.

Over time, you will notice that your strongest qualities may have been hidden beneath layers of doubt. Resilience uncovers them. It teaches you to keep going after each knockdown, to adjust your sails when the winds change, and to celebrate small wins along the way. In doing so, you become a light for others who feel lost.

As you continue building your business and walking in faith, keep resilience close to your heart. Use the practices and tools from this chapter to nurture a mindset that refuses to quit. Draw comfort from the knowledge that God stands with you. Ask for help, both from people around you and from a higher power. Step by step, you will transform challenges into stepping stones and setbacks into lessons.

Resilient thinking does not promise a life free of trouble. It promises that troubles will not break you. You will bend, sway, and maybe lose a branch or two, but your roots in faith will hold you upright. The next time you face a fierce storm—whether in business or in life—remember: you are capable of bouncing back. The best is yet to come when you master the art of resilient thinking.

PART III

THE JOURNEY OF FAITH IN ACTION

06

NAVIGATING FEAR AND DOUBT

"For God has not given us a spirit of fear, but of power and of love and of a sound mind."

(2 TIMOTHY 1:7)

Facing the Shadows

Imagine you are on a path through the woods. The sun filters through leaves, and birds sing overhead. It seems peaceful—until you hear a rustling sound nearby. You freeze, heart pounding, uncertain what might leap out at you. In business and in life, that rustling can represent your fears and doubts. They creep up unexpectedly, making your mind race with "what if" questions. You might think, "What if my idea fails?" "What if people laugh at me?" or "What if I am not good enough?"

Fear and doubt are like shadows that follow you along your journey. They may not go away entirely, but you can learn to walk forward in spite of them. In this chapter, you will discover practical steps to face fear and doubt head-on. You will see how faith can shine a light when you feel uncertain and how simple shifts in your thinking can help you move forward with courage.

I remember a time when I was about to speak at an important event. My heart raced, and I kept picturing the worst outcomes: forgetting my words, boring the audience, or stumbling on stage. Even though I had practiced a lot, doubt ate at me. It felt like a heavy weight in my chest. But as I prayed and leaned on the support of friends, I found a calm place inside myself. I reminded myself why my message mattered. Overcoming that wave of fear did not happen all at once—it happened by taking small steps forward, even with my legs trembling.

By the end of this chapter, you will have a clearer view of what fear and doubt are, why they show up, and how you can keep going despite them. You will also see how leaning on your faith can turn your worries into moments of breakthrough. Fear may never fully vanish, but it can learn to stand aside while you continue on your path, guided by purpose and hope.

Understanding Fear and Doubt

Fear and doubt are natural human emotions. They come from the part of your brain that wants to keep you safe. Long ago, fear was useful when people had to watch for dangerous animals or enemy tribes. Doubt could help you pause before making risky choices. Even now, fear can protect you from real danger—like touching a hot stove or stepping too close to a ledge. Doubt can make you think twice before investing your life savings in a random idea.

However, when it comes to your business dreams or personal growth, fear and doubt often grow bigger than they need to be. They can show up like giant roadblocks, warning you to turn back even when the road ahead is not truly dangerous. You might say, "I cannot risk everything on a new product," or "I doubt my skills," or "I do not deserve success." These thoughts can stop you from even trying.

The first step in handling fear and doubt is to understand that they are not always telling the truth. Sometimes, they are based on old beliefs or scary stories you have heard. Sometimes, they come from a single failure you had in the past, which makes you think you will always fail. Recognizing that your fear may be an overreaction can help you see past it.

In business, fear often pops up when you are about to do something new: launching a website, speaking in front of customers, or investing in a project. Doubt whispers, "What if you look foolish? What if this fails?" The reality is, you might look foolish, or you might fail. But those outcomes are not the end of your journey. They are experiences you can learn from.

Think of fear and doubt like backseat drivers in your car. They might shout warnings and instructions, but you are the one who decides where to steer. You can acknowledge their presence without letting them control your actions. That is the essence of navigating fear and doubt: listening to the warnings, taking what is helpful, and then calmly driving forward with faith as your compass.

Identifying Your Core Fears

One way to stand up to fear is to name it. When you feel nervous or uneasy, pause and ask, "What exactly am I afraid of?" You might discover common fears such as:

Fear of Failure

This fear says, "If I fail, I will look foolish. People will judge me." It might also whisper, "I cannot handle the disappointment." But remember that failing once does not make you a failure. It means you tried something and it did not work out—this time. You can try again or try differently.

Fear of Success

It sounds strange, but some people are scared of actually succeeding. They worry about the pressure that comes with growth or the higher expectations from others. They might think, "What if I cannot keep this up?" or "I am not worthy of success." Recognizing this fear can free you to enjoy the blessings that come when things go right.

Fear of Rejection

In business, you might approach potential clients or investors and risk hearing "no." This can feel like a personal blow: "They do not like me." But in truth, rejection often has nothing to do with your worth.

Sometimes, the timing is off or the other person's needs do not match your offer. A "no" can be a stepping stone to a better "yes" down the road.

Fear of the Unknown

Starting a new venture can be scary because there are so many question marks. You do not know how people will respond or if the market will change. This fear makes you want to stay in your comfort zone. However, growth almost always involves stepping into the unknown.

Fear of Letting People Down

Maybe you have a family that depends on you, or employees who trust your leadership. The thought of disappointing them can be a heavy weight. Yet, part of leadership is making tough calls. Not every decision will please everyone, but doing nothing out of fear can lead to worse outcomes.

By naming the specific fear, you shrink its power. You move from general anxiety ("I am scared!") to a clearer statement ("I am worried about failing in front of my boss"). Once the fear is defined, you can explore if it is realistic and figure out healthy ways to address it. Sometimes, you will see the fear is much bigger in your mind than in reality. Other times, you will realize, "This fear is telling me I need more preparation," or "I should find a mentor to guide me." Clarity is the first step toward action.

The Sneaky Nature of Doubt

Doubt often works more quietly than fear. While fear can shout warnings, doubt whispers questions: "Are you sure you can handle this? Do you really know what you are doing?" It can sit in the back of your mind and eat away at your confidence. Over time, it might stop you from taking even small risks.

Sometimes, doubt appears when you compare yourself to others. You see someone else succeeding and think, "They are so talented. I will never be that good." Or you see a smooth presentation by a business leader and assume they never feel scared. Yet behind the scenes, everyone experiences moments of doubt. They just learn to work through it.

Doubt can also show up when you make a plan but second-guess every detail. Instead of moving forward, you endlessly tweak your approach. While careful planning is wise, too much hesitation can stall you. You might keep your business idea a secret for years because you never feel "ready." The truth is, you will rarely feel 100% ready.

Another form of doubt is imposter syndrome. This is when you achieve success or recognition, but deep down, you think you do not deserve it. You worry someone will find out you are "faking it." This can make you afraid to speak up or take on bigger roles. But remember that learning is part of the journey. Nobody knows everything. Even experts keep growing their skills.

To tackle doubt, first notice when it creeps in. Then, ask if there is real evidence for this doubt. Did you truly underperform, or did you just make one small mistake? Have people given you positive feedback, but you brushed it off? Collect real facts. Often, the facts show you are more capable than you give yourself credit for. You might also talk to a trusted friend or mentor who can remind you of your strengths. Hearing someone else's perspective can cut through the fog of doubt.

Faith's Role in Overcoming Fear and Doubt

Faith can act like a lantern when you are walking through a dark forest of unknowns. When you trust in God (or your higher power), you remember that you do not have to figure out everything by yourself. You can pray for wisdom, courage, and clarity. While this does not guarantee you will avoid hard times, it does mean you have a steady hand guiding you.

Believing in something greater than yourself can transform your view of fear and doubt. Instead of seeing them as unbeatable forces, you see them as challenges that can grow your character. In times of uncertainty, you might say, "God, I feel unsure, but I believe You are with me." This simple act can calm the inner storm, giving you room to think clearly.

Faith also reminds you that your identity is not solely tied to your success or failure. You are more than your job title, bank account, or follower count. Even if a project collapses, you still have worth as a loved creation. This bigger perspective can shrink the power of fear that says, "If I fail, I am nothing." No—if you fail, you are still you, with the chance to try again.

Another way faith helps is by teaching you about purpose. Fear thrives when you see no meaning in your struggles. But if you believe your work has a calling behind it—to serve others, to spread kindness, to honor your gifts—then fear and doubt become bumps in a road that leads somewhere important. You can say, "I am facing these challenges for a reason, and I will keep going."

When I launched my first product, I felt waves of fear. Sales were slow, and I imagined worst-case scenarios. But each day, I prayed, "God, show me the right path. Help me help people with this idea." I slowly shifted from "Oh no, what if I fail?" to "How can I serve others with what I have?" That faith-based shift in mindset carried me through tough moments and eventually led me to pivot my product in a way that finally connected with customers.

Practical Ways to Confront Fear

Sometimes, the best way to shrink fear is to face it head-on. Here are some simple strategies to consider:

Set Small Goals

If the big picture scares you, break it down. Want to open a bakery? Instead of quitting your job tomorrow, start by testing recipes at home. Then, sell them at a local market. Each small step proves you can move forward without chaos.

Do a "Worst-Case Scenario" Exercise

Sit down with a notebook and write out the absolute worst thing that could happen. Maybe you lose money or get negative feedback. Then, ask yourself how you would recover. Often, you discover that even the worst-case scenario is not as awful as your mind makes it out to be.

Use Positive Self-Talk

Catch negative thoughts and replace them. If you think, "I cannot do this," say instead, "This will be challenging, but I can learn." It might feel cheesy at first, but words have power. Over time, they reshape your inner dialogue.

Find a Fear Buddy

Share your fear with a friend or mentor. Let them encourage you. Sometimes, just saying your fear out loud robs it of much of its strength. They might also give you practical tips or a reminder of times you have succeeded before. Keep in mind you want someone that will also be honest and look for the positive rather than the negative. You can find negative everywhere.

Practice Brave Moments

Train your "fear muscle" by regularly doing small things that scare you. This could be speaking up in a meeting, introducing yourself to a new person, or trying a new hobby. Each time you succeed, you build confidence for the bigger leaps.

Pray or Meditate

Before a scary step, take a few moments to breathe deeply and center yourself. If you pray, say, "God, thank You for being with me. Please calm my mind." If you meditate, picture yourself handling the situation with calmness and grace.

These methods do not make fear vanish instantly, but they give you tools to handle it. Overcoming fear is often a process of repeated small actions. Each time you face your fear, you realize you are stronger than you thought. You also gather experiences that help you challenge fear the next time it arises.

Doubt-Busting Techniques

Doubt can be sneaky, so having a handful of doubt-busting techniques can keep it from taking root in your mind.

Track Your Wins

Keep a journal or a digital note where you record each positive result. It could be as simple as landing a small client or receiving a kind compliment. Reviewing these "wins" can remind you of your competence on days when doubt roars.

Check the Facts

If you doubt your skills, gather real evidence. Did you finish a major project? Do people often thank you for your work? If yes, that is proof you can do it. Facts can pierce through the fog of "I am not good enough."

Seek Honest Feedback

Ask a trusted person, "Where do you see my strengths and weaknesses?" A balanced view helps you see areas you truly need to improve and areas you are already strong in. Doubt often thrives on vague feelings. Feedback can provide clear direction.

Embrace Imperfection

Sometimes, doubt says you have to be perfect before you try. That is impossible. Perfection is a moving target. Recognize that mistakes are part of growth. If you slip up, learn the lesson, adjust, and move on. Doubt loses its grip when you accept that you are always in a state of learning.

Visualize Success

Spend a few minutes imagining yourself completing a tough task successfully. Picture the steps, how it feels, and the positive outcome. By rehearsing success in your mind, you build a sense of "I can handle this."

Scripture and Affirmations

If you come from a faith tradition, certain verses or passages might speak directly against doubt. Keep them handy. If you are not religious, affirmations can work similarly. Repeat short, uplifting statements like, "I am capable, and I trust the process."

In my own life, doubt often showed up when I was trying something new, like creating a training program. My mind would say, "You do not know enough to teach others." To bust that doubt, I listed the past experiences that qualified me—like successful projects, feedback from people I had mentored, and certifications I had earned. Seeing that list reminded me I did have something valuable to share. Step by step, I learned to trust my abilities, and the training program ended up helping many people.

When Fear and Doubt Are Telling You Something Important

Not all fear and doubt are unhelpful. Sometimes, these emotions serve as an alarm bell. For instance, if you are about to invest all your savings in a questionable scheme, a healthy level of fear might make you pause and do more research. Or if you are about to partner with someone whose values clash with yours, a nudge of doubt might be warning you to proceed carefully.

The challenge is separating the helpful warnings from the unwarranted panic. You can do this by examining the source of your fear or doubt:

Check Past Experiences:

Have you or someone you trust been burned in a similar situation? If so, your fear might be a signal to slow down and investigate more thoroughly.

Seek Counsel:

Talk to someone with more experience. If they confirm your worries are valid, you might need to change your plan. If they say your fears seem unfounded, you can proceed with more confidence.

Pray or Reflect:

Ask God for clarity or spend quiet time listening to your intuition. Sometimes, you get a strong sense of peace or a "red flag" feeling. Trust those signals, but also balance them with practical wisdom.

Use Logic:

Lay out the pros and cons on paper. If your fear stems from real disadvantages, that is important to note. If the cons are mostly "what if" scenarios without much basis, it might be fear out of proportion.

I once considered bringing on a business partner who had a flashy presentation but not much proven track record. My excitement told me to sign fast. But I felt a small flicker of doubt—something felt off. I prayed for clarity, then researched more. I found that he had a history of broken promises with past partners. That doubt ended up saving me from a problematic deal. Not every doubt is your enemy; sometimes it is a friend trying to protect you.

The Connection Between Fear, Doubt, and Stress

Fear and doubt can feed into stress, especially when you run a busy business or juggle many responsibilities. Stress raises your heart rate, tenses your muscles, and clouds your mind. When you are stressed, fear can feel more overwhelming, and doubt can twist every little worry into a huge concern.

Recognize the Signs:

If you notice you are constantly feeling exhausted or cranky, or you keep having headaches and trouble sleeping, stress might be growing. This, in turn, can worsen your fear and doubt, creating a cycle. You might start thinking, "I cannot handle all this!" which multiplies your anxiety.

Break the Cycle:

One way to disrupt this cycle is through stress management. Simple practices like deep breathing, a short walk, or a quick stretch break can calm your body. When your body relaxes, your mind can think more clearly. You might also schedule short times for prayer or positive reading during the day. This mini "reset" can lower stress levels before they spiral.

Time Management:

A big source of stress is feeling like there is too much to do and not enough time. Learning to prioritize can help. If you tackle the most important tasks first, you reduce the stress of looming deadlines. This also helps with doubt because you see real progress on important goals.

Ask for Help:

Do not be afraid to delegate tasks or lean on others. Building a team, even if it is just a few reliable people, can lighten your load. When fear and doubt say, "You must do everything yourself," remind yourself that collaboration is wise, not weak.

By keeping stress in check, you create a healthier environment for your mind. You give yourself breathing room to face fear and doubt with logic and faith. You also preserve your energy for the tasks that truly matter, rather than spending it on constant worry. Over time, a less stressed mind is more open to possibility and better able to see creative solutions hiding behind fear.

Personal Testimony—A Leap of Faith

I want to share a personal story about a time I confronted fear and doubt head-on. A few years ago, I had a decent job, steady pay, and a comfortable routine. Yet, there was a dream in my heart to start a coaching business. The thought of leaving my safe position made my stomach churn. Fear's voice said, "What if you fail and lose everything?" Doubt chimed in, "You are not qualified enough to coach anyone."

For months, I wrestled with these feelings. I prayed constantly, asking, "God, is this dream from You, or is it just my wild imagination?" Little by little, I felt a growing peace about taking the risk. I started by coaching a few people on weekends to test my skills. Their positive feedback showed me I did have something to offer. My confidence grew as I gathered real evidence.

Finally, I took the leap. I left my job and poured my energy into the coaching business. The first six months were terrifying. My income was not stable. My schedule felt chaotic as I learned marketing, client management, and bookkeeping. But each time fear told me to give up, I remembered why I started. Each time doubt told me I was an imposter, I looked at testimonials from clients who said I helped them improve.

Over time, the business found its footing. I learned to set realistic goals, partner with other entrepreneurs, and adapt my services to what people truly needed. Looking back, I see that my fear and doubt did not disappear. They were still there, but they no longer had the final say. Faith, along with steady effort, guided me through the rough patches. Today, that coaching business is thriving, and it never would have existed if I had let fear and doubt keep me in my comfort zone.

Leaning on Community and Support

Facing fear and doubt alone can be overwhelming. That is why having a supportive community can make all the difference. You might join a networking group of fellow entrepreneurs, a church group, or an online forum where people discuss challenges openly. Talking with others who have faced similar fears helps you see you are not alone.

Family and Friends:

Share your dreams with people close to you. Let them know where you feel shaky. Often, they will offer a listening ear or a kind word that lifts your spirits. Be sure to choose people who are likely to be encouraging rather than negative. Not everyone will get your vision, but some will stand by you no matter what.

Mentors and Role Models:

Look for someone who has succeeded in an area you care about. Ask if they can offer guidance. Sometimes, just hearing their story of overcoming fear can spark your own courage. A good mentor can point out blind spots, cheer your wins, and gently challenge you to grow.

Professional Help:

If your fear and doubt feel unmanageable, there is no shame in seeking help from a counselor or therapist. They are trained to help you untangle harmful thought patterns and create healthier coping strategies. Many business leaders quietly see therapists to handle stress and fear so they can lead more effectively.

Give and Receive Support:

Community is about give-and-take. When you hear someone else's fears, you can encourage them. This also reminds you of your own progress. Sharing your personal victories and lessons can help someone else see that fear is not unbeatable. And when you are the one feeling low, others can return the favor.

I remember joining a local business meetup during my first year of full-time entrepreneurship. I felt insecure walking into a room of confident-looking people. But as I started talking, I realized many of them were just as unsure behind the smiles. Over coffee chats, we shared war stories of lost clients and long nights of self-doubt. Knowing I was not the only one fighting this battle gave me strength to keep going.

Turning Fear and Doubt into Fuel

Sometimes, the very things that scare you can become motivation. If you are afraid of letting your family down, transform that fear into dedication: "I will work smarter and ask for help so I can provide for them." If you doubt your knowledge, use that as a push to study, take courses, or practice more. Fear and doubt can act like alarm clocks, waking you up to areas where you need to grow.

Reframe the Emotion:

Instead of saying, "I am terrified," say, "I am feeling energized for a challenge." This does not mean you deny that you are scared. You simply relabel the emotion in a way that helps you act. The adrenaline that comes with fear can sharpen your mind if you channel it toward problem-solving.

Set Stretch Goals:

A stretch goal is one that lies just outside your comfort zone. If your fear says, "You can only handle small tasks," set a slightly bigger goal—one that challenges you but is not impossible. Reaching that stretch goal shows you can handle more than you thought, building confidence.

Celebrate Micro-Wins:

Every time you push past fear or doubt, even in a small way, acknowledge it. Maybe you introduced yourself at a conference instead of hiding in the corner. Maybe you sent an email to a potential client you thought would say no. Each tiny act of bravery is proof you are capable of growth.

Reflect on Progress:

Schedule moments to look back on how far you have come. If you keep a journal, read old entries about your worries. You might be amazed at how things turned out better than you expected. This reflection can turn your fear into gratitude and your doubt into action.

One of my greatest leaps came when I realized my fear could be the energy I needed to get started each day. Instead of waiting until I "felt ready," I started my mornings by praying, then tackling one task that scared me. This could be writing a blog post on a topic I was not fully sure about or calling a new lead. Over time, the tasks got less scary because I had evidence that I could handle them. Fear became a signal that I was moving into new territory—exactly where growth happens.

Overcoming Fear and Doubt in the Long Term

Fear and doubt do not vanish after one victory. They might return whenever you face bigger challenges. That is normal. What matters is creating a lifestyle that continually addresses these emotions in a healthy way.

Maintain a Growth Mindset:

Remind yourself that every skill can improve with practice, every setback can teach, and every success can open the door for the next level. This outlook keeps fear from paralyzing you and doubt from defining you.

Continue Learning:

Invest in courses, books, private sessions or workshops. Staying updated in your field reduces fear because you feel more prepared. When doubt says, "You do not know enough," you can say, "I am committed to learning."

Stay Connected to Faith:

Keep prayer, worship, or meditation as part of your regular routine. This connection grounds you and offers peace that goes beyond human logic. It reassures you that you are never walking alone, even when you feel shaky.

Evaluate Your Environment:

Surround yourself with people, media, and habits that lift you up. If a certain online group or TV show constantly feeds worry and negativity, consider cutting back. Instead, fill your mental space with hopeful voices and success stories.

Set New Challenges Regularly:

As you conquer old fears, set fresh challenges. This does not mean you never rest—it means you do not let yourself get too comfortable. Growth happens at the edge of your comfort zone, where new fears appear and can be conquered in turn.

Remember Past Victories:

On days when fear or doubt returns in full force, recall how you over-came them before. If you made it through once, you can do it again, maybe even faster this time. You have experience and wisdom you did not have earlier.

I still deal with fear and doubt whenever I consider launching a new project or scaling up my work. But now, I know the process: I pray, I name the fear, I gather facts, and I take brave steps anyway. Instead of expecting fear to vanish, I expect it to show up—and I meet it like an old acquaintance, saying, "Hello again. I am going forward anyway." That mindset shift has helped me keep growing in both my business and personal life.

Walking Forward with Courage

Fear and doubt are not monsters meant to stop you forever. They are signals that something new or challenging lies ahead. You can let these signals scare you off the path, or you can face them, learn from them, and keep walking. By shining the light of faith, truth, and community support on your worries, you discover that many of them lose their power.

The journey to overcome fear and doubt is not a one-time event—it is a life-long practice. Each time you step beyond your comfort zone, you show yourself that growth is possible. Each time you let faith guide you, you prove you do not have to do it alone. Every lesson learned from mistakes and successes becomes part of your story, one that you can share to help others navigate their own fears and doubts.

Take a moment right now to imagine the future you want. What if you moved forward despite your doubts? What if you took that brave step? Let hope spark in your heart. The road ahead might still have twists and turns, but you have the tools to handle them. You know how to name your fears, question your doubts, lean on faith, and tap into support. This is how you navigate fear and doubt without letting them rob you of your destiny.

So go ahead—take that next small step. Press send on the email, sign up for the class, make the phone call, share your idea. The more you act, the more courage grows. And when fear or doubt whisper in your ear again, you can smile and say, "I hear you, but I am moving forward anyway." Let that be your daily practice: not to wait until you are fearless, but to keep going even when fear and doubt ride along as passengers. Over time, you will find they stay quiet in the backseat while you, guided by faith, steer toward a future filled with possibility.

07

OVERCOMING OBSTACLES WITH SPIRITUAL TOOLS

*"The LORD will fight for you; you
need only to be still."*

(EXODUS 14:14)

Turning Challenges into Opportunities

Picture a winding road with steep hills and sharp turns. You start your journey with excitement, but soon you face bumpy patches that slow you down. Obstacles pop up at every corner, making you wonder if you are on the right path. In business and in life, these obstacles can feel overwhelming. They might be financial hardships, conflicts with partners, or fear that you are not qualified enough. Sometimes, you may want to throw up your hands and say, "This is just too hard!"

Yet, there is another way to see these roadblocks. What if each obstacle was also a chance to learn, grow, and draw closer to a higher power? What if you had spiritual tools that could lift your perspective and show you a path forward? In this chapter, you will discover how to use prayer, meditation, and other faith-based practices to handle life's challenges with courage and wisdom. You will see that obstacles do not have to stop your progress. They can become steppingstones leading to deeper strength and success.

I remember a time when my business felt stuck. My savings were running low, and my biggest client decided to move on. Fear gripped my heart, and I could hardly sleep at night. Then, a wise mentor reminded me of the power of prayer and reflection. Instead of trying to force a solution, I spent time each morning asking God for guidance. Slowly, fresh ideas appeared. I noticed doors opening in areas I never thought to look before. That is the power of spiritual tools: they do not always fix your problems overnight, but they open your eyes to new possibilities and bring peace in the middle of storms.

By the end of this chapter, you will learn how to use spiritual tools like prayer, meditation, scripture reading, journaling, and forgiveness practices to move through difficult times. You will find that turning upward, inward, and outward for help can re-energize your mind, renew your heart, and lead you to solutions you might have never considered. Whether you are facing a major crisis or a small setback, these tools will help you stand firm, ready to meet the challenge. Let us begin this journey of discovering how faith can transform obstacles into opportunities for growth.

Recognizing Obstacles as Part of Growth

When you start a new project or embark on a dream, you may hope for smooth sailing. But life rarely works that way. Obstacles often show up, blocking the path or making it bumpy. It can be easy to see these obstacles as signs that you should quit. You might think, "Maybe this is a message to stop." However, many spiritual traditions teach that challenges can be part of the plan to help you grow stronger, wiser, and more compassionate.

Embracing the Learning Process

It helps to think of your business or personal journey like a classroom. Each obstacle is a lesson. If you avoid the lessons, you might end up repeating the same problems again and again. If you face them with curiosity, asking questions like, "What can I learn here?" or "How can this make me better?" you begin to grow. Just as your muscles get stronger by lifting heavier weights, your inner strengths can grow by overcoming bigger challenges.

The Bigger Picture

Faith offers a bigger picture of life. Instead of seeing one hard moment as the end, you see it as a chapter in a much larger story. You trust that even when things feel unfair or impossible, there may be a higher purpose unfolding. Maybe this obstacle shows you a mistake in your plan, giving you a chance to correct it before it becomes bigger. Maybe it leads you to seek help from people who will become lifelong friends and supporters.

Real-World Example

I recall a small bakery owner who struggled with low sales. He felt discouraged and thought about closing shop. Yet, he decided to pray for fresh ideas. In time, he realized his community needed gluten-free and vegan options—something he had never considered before. By adding these items, his bakery became a local favorite for people with special diets. Without the initial obstacle, he might never have discovered this untapped market. His faith and openness turned a problem into a stepping stone.

When you recognize obstacles as part of growth, you are less likely to give up or feel hopeless. You may not welcome challenges with open arms, but you will not fear them as much. Instead, you develop a sense of trust that each hurdle can teach you or lead you to a better path.

The Power of Prayer in Tough Times

Prayer is one of the simplest and most common spiritual tools. It involves speaking to your higher power—often God—about your struggles, desires, or gratitude. But prayer is not just about presenting a wish list. It can also be a way to calm your mind, open your heart, and receive guidance.

Types of Prayer

Petitionary Prayer:

This is when you ask God for something, like wisdom or help resolving a conflict. You might say, "God, please guide me in finding the right solution. I feel stuck, and I need Your light."

Thanksgiving Prayer:

Even when life is hard, there is almost always something to be grateful for. You might thank God for your health, your family, or the resources you still have. Gratitude shifts your focus from what is lacking to what is present.

Confessional Prayer:

Sometimes, obstacles arise because of your own mistakes or attitudes. In this prayer, you admit where you went wrong or how you might have caused harm. Owning your part opens space for healing and change.

Listening Prayer:

This is a quieter form of prayer where you spend time in silence, waiting for insight. You are not actively asking for anything; you are simply being still, letting divine wisdom touch your thoughts.

How Prayer Helps

When fear or frustration consume you, prayer offers a sense of release. You hand over your worries to a loving presence, trusting that you are not alone in your struggles. This act often brings emotional relief. Many people also speak of receiving unexpected ideas or comfort during prayer—like a gentle whisper in their heart guiding them to the next step.

Prayer can also strengthen your bond with others. When you pray for your team members, employees, or partners, you develop empathy. You start caring more about their well-being. This fosters unity, which can be essential when tackling big hurdles together.

Practical Tips

- **Schedule Prayer Time:** Make it part of your daily routine, even if just for five minutes.
- **Journal Your Prayers:** Writing them down can help you track when prayers are answered or how your feelings change.
- **Pray with Others:** Gather a small group to pray about shared challenges. Hearing their voices can boost your faith.

In my life, prayer has changed many roadblocks into opportunities. I remember a time when I faced a financial crunch. Stress kept me awake at night. When I finally prayed, "God, give me the wisdom to manage my resources better," I felt calmer. Soon, I bumped into an old friend who was a financial advisor. He offered tips that helped me create a better budget. Coincidence? Maybe. But I believe prayer opened my eyes to help I might have otherwise ignored.

Meditation and Stillness for Inner Clarity

While prayer involves speaking or listening to God, meditation often focuses on stillness and mindfulness. Both are spiritual tools that can help you overcome life's obstacles. In meditation, you quiet the chatter of your mind, allowing a sense of peace to rise within you. This calmness can be a powerful weapon against stress, fear, and decision fatigue.

Different Ways to Meditate

1. **Breath-Focused Meditation:** Sit comfortably, close your eyes, and pay attention to your breathing. Feel the air go in and out of your nose. If thoughts wander, gently guide them back to your breath.
2. **Guided Visualization:** Imagine yourself in a peaceful place, like a garden or a beach. Picture any worries as clouds that drift away in the sky, leaving your mind clear.

3. **Scripture or Mantra Meditation:** If you have a favorite verse or phrase like "Peace, be still," repeat it silently to yourself. This repetition helps keep your mind from racing.

4. **Body Scan:** Focus on each part of your body, from your toes to your head. Notice tension and imagine it dissolving. This can ease stress and ground you in the present moment.

Benefits for Overcoming Obstacles

Meditation trains your mind to stay present. Obstacles often cause anxiety about the future or regrets about the past. When you meditate, you practice returning to the now. This helps you think more clearly about the issue at hand without spinning in circles of worry.

Meditation can also reduce the emotional charge of a problem. Instead of reacting impulsively out of anger or fear, you learn to respond thoughtfully. You might find a creative solution that was hidden under all the mental noise.

Combining Meditation and Faith

For many people, meditation is not just a standalone practice. They invite God (or their higher power) into their quiet time. They might start with a short prayer, "God, be with me in this stillness," and then settle into silence. This approach blends the best of both worlds—prayerful connection and deep internal peace.

One friend of mine used to have panic attacks whenever sales dropped. She started a five-minute meditation routine each morning, focusing on a comforting verse. Over a few weeks, she noticed she could handle dips in revenue with less fear. She felt more in control, more trusting that a solution would appear. That is the power of a calm and centered mind—it sees opportunities instead of just dangers.

Journaling as a Spiritual Practice

Journaling can be a bridge between your thoughts and your deeper wisdom. It is a simple act: take a pen and paper (or a keyboard although I think writing things down is more powerful) and write down whatever is on your mind. But this act can be incredibly powerful when facing obstacles because it helps you see patterns, release emotions, and invite spiritual insight into daily struggles.

Why Journaling Helps

- **Clarity:** When problems spin in your head, they can grow bigger and scarier. Writing them down makes them more concrete. You can examine each worry instead of feeling overwhelmed by a cloud of thoughts.
- **Honesty:** A journal is a private space. You can be fully honest about your fears, doubts, or even anger. Honesty often leads to breakthroughs, as you no longer hide from your own feelings.
- **Tracking Growth:** By reviewing old entries, you see how you have grown or how certain prayers were answered. This record builds your faith that future challenges can also be overcome.

Spiritual Journaling Techniques

- **Prayer Journal:**
  Write your prayers each day. Include thanks, requests, and feelings. Return to them later to see if or how your prayers were answered.

- **Reflection Prompts:**
  Choose prompts like, "What obstacle am I facing right now?" or "Where do I need divine guidance?" and write honestly for a few minutes. Let your thoughts flow.

- **Gratitude Pages:**

  At the end of each day, list three things you are thankful for. This balances stress with recognition of the good in your life.

- **Scripture or Devotional Response:**

  Read a short verse or faith-based quote, then write how it applies to your current obstacle. This invites spiritual wisdom into your problem-solving process.

Personal Example

When I was uncertain about expanding my business to a new city, I started journaling daily. Each morning, I wrote down my worries: "What if it costs too much? What if no one wants my services there?" I also listed possible solutions. Over time, I noticed repeating themes. Most of my fears were not about finances, but about leaving my comfort zone. That clarity helped me tackle my real issue: my fear of the unknown. I prayed specifically about that fear and found the courage to take the leap. The move ended up creating new opportunities I never thought possible.

Journaling can feel awkward at first, but even a few minutes a day can make a huge difference. It is a way to invite God (or your higher power) into your thought process while also uncovering truths about yourself. When facing obstacles, journaling becomes a faithful friend, always ready to listen and reflect back the path you seek.

Scripture, Sacred Texts, and Wisdom Teachings

For many believers, sacred texts offer guidance that goes beyond human reasoning. It might be the Bible, the Quran, or teachings from spiritual leaders. These texts often include stories of people who faced impossible odds, overcame great trials, or found hope in dire situations. By reading these accounts, you learn that life's biggest mountains can be moved through faith, perseverance, and divine help.

Applying Ancient Wisdom to Modern Problems

Find Relevant Passages:

If you are feeling fear, look for verses or stories about courage. If you are battling guilt, find sections on forgiveness. Tailoring your reading to your current challenge can bring fresh insights.

Interpret with an Open Heart:

While texts were written in different times, their core truths often apply to modern life. For example, a story about a shepherd facing a giant might speak to you about facing your own "giant" problems at work. Ask, "What lesson can I draw from this?"

Reflect or Meditate on the Passage:

After reading, sit quietly. Let the words soak in. How do they challenge or comfort you? This invites a deeper connection rather than just skimming through.

Share with Others:

Discuss verses or stories with a small group or a mentor. Hearing their perspectives can reveal truths you might have missed. Sometimes, a friend's insight can unlock a solution you never would have seen alone.

Inspiration and Hope

When you read stories of people who overcame obstacles by faith, it fuels your own belief that you can do the same. You see examples of patience and trust in the face of adversity. You learn that even heroes struggled with doubt, anger, or fear, yet they still found a way through.

I remember being moved by the story of Moses leading people through the wilderness. They faced countless hardships—lack of food, complaints, and even rebellion. Yet, Moses kept going, guided by faith. When my own leadership felt overwhelming, I recalled how Moses turned to prayer and wise counsel. If he could lead thousands through unknown territory with God's help, maybe I could lead my small team through our own challenges. The story became a source of steady confidence.

Practicing Forgiveness to Clear the Path

When you carry resentment, anger, or blame, it can weigh you down. These negative feelings can become invisible obstacles, blocking new blessings or creative ideas. Forgiveness is not about saying someone's hurtful action was okay. It is about releasing the burden so you can move forward without bitterness.

Why Forgiveness Is a Spiritual Tool

- **Emotional Healing:** Refusing to forgive keeps wounds open. Forgiveness allows you to start healing.
- **Clarity in Decision-Making:** Anger can cloud your judgment. By letting go of grudges, you free up mental space to tackle real problems.
- **Better Relationships:** Business thrives on trust and cooperation. Holding grudges against team members or partners can sabotage future success. Forgiveness paves the way for healthier teamwork.
- **Alignment with Higher Principles:** Many faiths teach compassion and grace. Practicing forgiveness aligns you with these spiritual ideals, creating harmony in your heart.

Steps to Forgive

Acknowledge the Hurt:

Name what happened and how it made you feel. Pretending it was no big deal does not promote true forgiveness.

Consider the Other Person's Perspective:

This does not excuse their action, but it might help you see they, too, were acting out of fear, ignorance, or their own pain.

Release the Burden:

You can say a prayer or a statement like, "I choose to forgive. I release this anger. I will not let it control me." Sometimes, writing a letter you never send helps.

Set Boundaries If Needed:

Forgiveness does not mean you must stay in a harmful situation. You can forgive someone and still choose to work or live apart if trust cannot be rebuilt yet.

Seek Divine Strength:

True forgiveness can be hard on your own. Ask God for help. Pray, "Give me the strength to forgive as You forgive."

Personal Reflection

I once had a business partner who broke my trust by stealing clients for his new firm. I felt betrayed. My anger consumed me for months. During that time, I noticed I could not focus on my own plans. My mind kept spinning on his wrongdoing. Finally, a friend suggested I pray about forgiveness. It was not easy. I had to do it again and again, each time I felt the anger well up. But over time, my heart softened. I let go of the grudge. Amazingly, once I released that anger, fresh ideas for my business came rushing in. Forgiveness cleared the emotional clutter, allowing room for new growth.

Building Community Support and Fellowship

Business problems and personal struggles can feel isolating. You might believe no one else understands your pain or that you must solve everything alone. But faith traditions teach the value of community—people who walk alongside you, pray with you, and offer support during tough times.

Different Forms of Spiritual Community

Small Groups or Prayer Circles:

These can meet at a church, community center, or even online. Members share their challenges and pray for one another. They celebrate victories and lift each other up during failures.

Mentorship Relationships:

A mentor who shares your faith can guide you both practically and spiritually. They might show you how to integrate business wisdom with deeper values.

Virtual Communities:

Online forums, social media groups, or faith-based webinars can connect you with people worldwide. If you live in an area without many in-person groups, this can be a great option.

Service Teams or Volunteer Groups:

Working together to help others—feeding the homeless, supporting a charity, or teaching a skill—can bond people in unexpected ways. You unite around a common cause and witness how helping others often eases your own burdens.

Why Fellowship Matters for Overcoming Obstacles

- **Shared Wisdom:** You learn from others' mistakes and breakthroughs.
- **Emotional Support:** Having someone who listens without judgment can relieve stress.
- **Accountability:** You stay committed to solutions because others check in on you.
- **Spiritual Strength:** Group prayer and worship can elevate hope, making problems seem more manageable.

When I lost a key client, a small group from my church prayed with me for new opportunities. One person introduced me to someone in a different industry. That connection led to a collaboration far beyond what I imagined. Had I kept my struggle hidden, I would have missed that blessing. Community support is not just about emotional comfort—it often brings practical help, too.

Spiritual Problem-Solving in Action

Let us walk through a simple, step-by-step example of how you might use spiritual tools to tackle a tough obstacle. Imagine you have a product launch that keeps getting delayed because of supply chain issues. You are losing money and patience. You feel anxious and frustrated.

Pause and Pray (or Meditate):

Before making a rash decision or lashing out at suppliers, take a moment. Find a quiet space. Ask God to calm your heart and grant wisdom. Or, if you prefer meditation, focus on your breath until you feel more centered.

Name the Problem in Your Journal:

Write down what is happening. Note how you feel: "I am worried about going broke," or "I am angry at the supplier." Identifying emotions can keep them from overwhelming you.

Seek Insight from Scripture or Spiritual Readings:

You might recall a story about patience or perseverance. Let that remind you that quick fixes are not always the answer. Patience can be part of the solution.

Brainstorm Creative Solutions:

With a calmer mind, list possible actions: finding a secondary supplier, scaling back the product line, or shifting your launch date. Let spiritual reflection guide you to think outside the box. Maybe a volunteer or friend from your community can help you find a new vendor.

Pray for Guidance on Each Option:

As you consider each path, ask for clarity: "Is this choice aligned with my values? Will it serve the people who need my product?"

Act and Trust the Process:

Pick the best option and move forward, trusting that you are not alone in this. Continue praying or meditating each day for ongoing direction.

Evaluate and Adjust:

Obstacles are rarely solved in one step. Stay open to signs that you need to tweak your plan. Keep your journal updated with progress, setbacks, and any blessings that appear.

By combining faith and practical problem-solving, you transform a scary situation into a journey of growth. Your spiritual tools anchor your emotions and expand your view of what is possible. Challenges may remain, but you move through them with purpose, not just panic.

Real-Life Stories of Triumph Through Faith

The Overworked Manager

A friend of mine managed a team in a busy tech company. She felt overwhelmed and worried she was failing her team. Each night, she prayed for guidance, asking God to show her how to delegate and trust others. Slowly, she let go of her need to micromanage. She even started a quick group prayer before meetings (for those who wanted it). Morale improved, and her team members became more confident. Her workload became lighter, not because the tasks vanished, but because she led with faith and let others step up.

The Struggling Student Entrepreneur

A college student I mentored dreamed of launching an app but had no money for developers. After weeks of frustration, he began daily meditations and reflection on a few encouraging verses. One day, he felt a nudge to join a local coding club. There, he met a group of peers who helped him build the first version of his app. They became co-founders, sharing the workload and eventual profits. His spiritual practice calmed his mind enough to notice the right opportunity.

The Healing of Relationships

A bakery owner had a falling-out with her sister, who had once been her partner. Their argument drained her focus and hurt her business. In church, she felt convicted to practice forgiveness. She wrote a heartfelt letter to her sister, apologizing for her own harsh words and offering a chance to reconcile. They did not become partners again, but they found peace and mutual support. The bakery owner's heart felt lighter. She could pour energy into her bakery instead of nursing anger. Within months, her sales soared, and she credited the shift to letting go of emotional burdens.

These stories show that spiritual tools—prayer, meditation, forgiveness, community support—can spark real change. Obstacles may not vanish instantly, but they become doors to deeper wisdom, stronger relationships, and unexpected breakthroughs. Each story proves that when you combine faith with action, amazing outcomes can unfold.

Creating Your Personal Toolbox

Now that you have read about various spiritual tools, it is time to build your own personal toolbox for overcoming obstacles. Just like a carpenter chooses the right tool for each job, you can select the practice that suits each situation or even combine several:

1. Daily Prayer or Meditation Routine

Carve out at least five minutes in the morning or evening to talk to God or quiet your mind. Consistency helps you stay spiritually grounded.

2. Regular Journaling Sessions

Choose a time each day or week to capture your thoughts, fears, and hopes on paper. Use prompts if you get stuck.

3. Scripture or Sacred Text Study

Set aside a small block of time to read meaningful passages. Keep notes on how they apply to your life.

4. Forgiveness Check

Every so often, ask yourself if you are harboring anger or resentment. If so, work through forgiveness steps before bitterness grows.

5. Community Involvement

Join or create a group that meets regularly to share struggles and wins. Offer to pray for each other or exchange helpful resources.

6. Service or Volunteer Work

Find a way to give back. Serving others can put your problems in perspective and fill you with renewed purpose.

7. Mentorship or Accountability Partner

Look for someone you trust—maybe a leader in your faith community—to hold you accountable for how you handle challenges.

8. Family Prayer or Discussion

If you have a family open to faith, encourage them to discuss daily obstacles together, praying or brainstorming solutions.

Make It Your Own

There is no single "right" way to use these tools. Some days, you might lean on prayer more heavily; other days, journaling might unlock the insight you need. The key is to remain flexible and open. As your life changes, your spiritual practices can adapt. The important thing is that you keep these tools handy, ready to be used whenever you face a wall.

Sustaining Faith Through Long-Term Challenges

Some obstacles vanish quickly—a small misunderstanding with a coworker or a minor setback in scheduling. But others can drag on for months or years, like a difficult financial season or a prolonged illness. In these situations, spiritual tools become even more crucial. They sustain you when you feel worn out.

The Nature of Endurance

Endurance means staying hopeful and active in the face of ongoing trouble. It does not mean ignoring the pain or stress. It means continuing to believe that relief or resolution can come, even if you do not see it yet. Spiritual tools can act like daily nourishment, feeding your soul so you do not give up.

- **Short Daily Prayers or Meditations:** Think of them as snacks for your spirit, keeping you fueled between major turning points.
- **Steady Journaling:** Record small victories—like a slightly improved cash flow or a moment of unexpected kindness from a client. These small positives keep you from drowning in the negative.
- **Leaning on Community:** If you face a long battle—say, dealing with chronic pain or a big legal conflict—keep your faith community updated. They can pray or offer assistance. Sometimes, just knowing people care can refresh your energy.
- **Checking Attitudes:** Over time, frustration can turn to bitterness or cynicism. Use prayer, meditation, or journaling to examine your heart. Are you drifting into despair? Ask God to renew your hope.

The Refining Process

Long-term challenges often refine your character. They teach deeper lessons of patience, empathy, and faithfulness. Think of gold being purified by fire. The heat is uncomfortable, but it removes impurities. If you let your spiritual tools do their work during these tough seasons, you will likely come out with a stronger spirit, better skills, and a more genuine heart.

I remember an 18-month stretch when I was weighed down by debt. Each time I felt close to clearing it, another expense popped up. I kept a scripture Philippians 4:19 - "And my God will meet all your needs according to the riches of His glory in Christ Jesus." on my fridge door about trusting God with my needs. Each morning, I read it and prayed for provision. Friends from my faith community occasionally gifted me groceries or offered side gigs. The journey was slow, but my trust in God's care deepened. By the time the debt was paid, I was not just relieved; I was transformed. My heart had grown more grateful, and my mind was sharper in handling finances. That is the power of enduring with spiritual help.

Choosing a Path of Faith in Every Obstacle

Obstacles are guaranteed in life and business. But how you face them makes all the difference. You can see them as final dead ends or as invitations to use your spiritual toolbox—prayer, meditation, scripture study, journaling, forgiveness, and community support. By choosing faith over fear, you open the door to solutions that might otherwise remain hidden.

As you leave this chapter, remember:

- **Obstacles Are Stepping Stones:** Each challenge can teach you or lead you to new insights.
- **Faith Provides Perspective:** Connecting with God helps you see beyond the immediate trouble, trusting that you are never alone.

- **Spiritual Tools Are Practical:** Prayer, meditation, and journaling are not airy ideas; they have real impact on your mindset and decisions.
- **Community Strengthens You:** Do not battle giants alone. Invite others to pray, advise, and walk with you.
- **Forgiveness Frees Your Mind and Heart:** Holding on to grudges only adds weight. Let forgiveness clear your path forward.
- **Long-Term Challenges Refine Character:** Even if your obstacle stretches out, keep leaning on faith for daily renewal.

The next time you face a daunting problem, pause. Take a deep breath. Consider which spiritual tool might help you find calm and wisdom. Pray for guidance. Write down your feelings in a journal. Reach out to a mentor or friend. And believe that the same power that carried people through storms thousands of years ago is still available to you today.

In the end, each challenge can become a chapter of growth in your larger story. By choosing a path of faith, you transform obstacles from threats into opportunities for transformation. May these spiritual tools serve you well, lighting your way when the road seems dark and guiding you toward solutions you never dreamed possible. Faith is not just a belief—it is a daily practice that lifts you above every barrier, showing you that with God's help, you can indeed overcome.

08

CONSISTENCY AND PERSEVERANCE

"And let us not grow weary of doing good, for in due season we will reap, if we do not give up."

(GALATIANS 6:9)

The Steady Beat That Carries You Forward

Think of a drum that keeps a steady beat in the background of a song. It is not flashy like a guitar solo or dramatic like a trumpet fanfare. But that steady drumbeat holds the entire piece of music together. In business and in life, consistency and perseverance act like that drumbeat. They might not always grab everyone's attention, but they create the rhythm that drives you toward your goals.

Every journey has days of sunshine and days of storm. On the bright days, you feel excited and motivated—you can almost taste success. But on stormy days, you might doubt yourself or wonder if you should give up. The secret to moving forward through both sun and storm is to keep marching steadily, day by day, step by step. This slow and steady progress might seem small, but over time, it leads to big results.

I recall a time when I tried to lose weight for health reasons. The first week, I felt super motivated, planning meals and going for walks. But after a while, I missed the snacks I used to enjoy, and early morning walks felt like a chore. A friend gave me great advice: "You do not have to do a lot each day—just do something every day." That simple tip taught me the power of sticking with small, consistent actions. Eventually, I saw real progress, and my energy returned. The same principle applies to building a business or pursuing any worthwhile goal.

In this chapter, you will learn how consistency and perseverance help you keep going long after the excitement fades. You will see how faith can fuel your determination and how small, daily habits can turn into major victories. You will also find practical tips to handle discouragement and develop a mindset that does not quit. By the end, you will have the tools to stay on your chosen path, even when the road feels long. Let us explore how a steady heart and unwavering spirit can carry you to success.

Perseverance—the Will to Keep Going

When Things Get Tough – which they will

If consistency is the daily action, perseverance is the spirit that keeps you from giving up when obstacles appear. It is the determination to keep marching, even when the trail is muddy or the weather is harsh. Perseverance kicks in when you face slow sales, skeptical clients, or personal setbacks that drain your energy. Instead of stopping, you push forward, trusting that the story is not over yet.

The Heart of Perseverance: Hope and Faith

Deep down, perseverance is about hope. You keep going because you believe your efforts will lead somewhere good. For many, faith in God strengthens that hope, reminding them that even in dark times, light can break through. Faith says, "I cannot see the end of the road, but I trust I am being guided. I will keep taking steps until the path becomes clear."

Biblical Examples: In the Bible, people like Noah or Moses continued onward despite huge challenges. They did not have all the answers, but they followed God's guidance one step at a time. Their perseverance led to remarkable outcomes.

Modern Inspirations: Today, you see stories of entrepreneurs who faced bankruptcy multiple times before finding success. They share how prayer or a strong belief in their calling kept them going.

The Rewards of Not Quitting

- **Stronger Character:** Each time you persevere, you stretch your limits and grow braver. Trials shape your character like fire refines gold.
- **Deeper Wisdom:** Problems teach valuable lessons about what works and what does not. If you quit too soon, you lose those insights.
- **Bigger Impact:** Perseverance can also inspire others. When your team or family sees you stand firm, they learn to do the same. You become a role model of dedication.

I once mentored a young entrepreneur who struggled with doubt. He tried many marketing tactics, but sales stayed low. He felt like giving up. Through regular chats, we prayed and reminded each other that seeds take time to grow. He stuck with his plan, adding small tweaks as he learned. Six months later, his sales began a steady climb. Now, he thanks that season of perseverance for teaching him grit. Without it, he might have abandoned his dream altogether.

Faith as the Backbone of Consistency and Perseverance

Why Faith Matters

You might wonder, "Is faith really necessary for staying consistent and persevering?" Not everyone has the same spiritual beliefs, yet for those who do, faith adds depth to their commitment. It reminds you that life is bigger than immediate gains. Even if business is slow, God can use this time to strengthen your character or open new doors. Faith puts setbacks in perspective, like clouds passing in a large sky.

Leaning on Prayer and Reflection

When your motivation feels drained, prayer and reflection can fill your tank. Spending quiet time each day—through prayer, scripture reading, or meditation—creates a stable foundation. It is like charging your phone battery each morning. No matter how chaotic the day gets, you have an internal power source that keeps you going.

- **Centering Your Mind:** During prayer, you can release worries and refocus on your purpose. Even five minutes of stillness can anchor you in hope and remind you why you began this journey.
- **Seeking Guidance:** Sometimes, problems feel too big for human wisdom alone. Faith teaches you to ask for divine wisdom. You might not hear a loud voice, but you might gain a quiet sense of peace or a hint of a new idea.

Trusting a Bigger Story

Faith also lets you see that your work has meaning beyond profit. Your commitment to consistency might bless someone who relies on your product or service. Your perseverance through a slump might inspire a teammate who is close to burning out. When you believe your efforts matter to God, you have extra reason to stay the course.

I remember a period when my small business faced one setback after another. It felt as though we took three steps backward for each step forward. In prayer, I found comfort in verses that spoke of endurance leading to hope. That sense of a bigger plan gave me the patience to keep trying. Eventually, we turned a corner, and our products began to resonate with customers. Looking back, I see how those trials refined our message and tested our resolve.

Practical Steps to Build Consistency

1. Set Clear, Achievable Goals

You cannot be consistent if you do not know what you are aiming for. Break down your big dreams into small steps. For instance, if you want to write a book, set a goal of writing 300 words each day. That might seem tiny, but over a year, it adds up to more than 100,000 words!

Make Goals Specific: "Write 300 words each day" is more tangible than "Work on my book sometimes."

Start Small: If 300 words still feels too big, write 150. The key is building a habit you can stick with, then raising the bar later.

2. Create Routines

Habits form best when attached to a regular time or place. You might decide that every weekday at 8 AM, you will tackle your most important project for 30 minutes. Once a habit is set, you spend less energy deciding what to do—you simply follow the routine.

Use Reminders: Alarms on your phone or notes on your fridge can help.

Batch Similar Tasks: Group tasks together so you can focus better. For instance, respond to emails from 9:00 to 9:30 each morning instead of checking them randomly all day.

3. Track Your Progress

Monitoring your actions can inspire you to keep going. You might keep a simple checklist or a daily journal. Seeing a streak of completed tasks builds momentum. If you miss a day, do not beat yourself up—start a new streak the next day.

Visual Tools: A wall calendar with checkmarks or stickers can motivate you.

Rewards: Give yourself small treats when you hit a milestone, like finishing a chapter or reaching 10 days of consistent work.

4. Overcome Procrastination

Procrastination is the enemy of consistency. If you find yourself delaying tasks, break them into smaller pieces. Promise yourself you will do just five minutes of the job. Often, once you start, you realize it is not so bad, and you continue. Also, reflect on your deeper reason for doing this task—maybe it is part of your calling or a way to serve others.

I once helped a friend who struggled to post weekly updates for her online shop. She felt overwhelmed by the thought of writing clever product descriptions each time. We agreed she would just draft one paragraph each Tuesday. That was it. Soon, she saw it only took about 15 minutes. After sticking with it for a couple of months, her shop gained followers who appreciated the consistent updates. Sometimes, the first step is half the battle.

How to Persevere When You Feel Like Quitting

Recognize Normal Cycles of Emotion

No one feels enthusiastic 24/7. Sometimes, your passion dips, or outside issues—like a family emergency—steal your focus. Accept that feeling down or discouraged is part of being human. Instead of saying, "I am failing because I do not feel super motivated," say, "This is a low point; how can I keep going anyway?"

Lean on Faith and Encouragement

When you are tempted to quit, it helps to talk with supportive friends, mentors, or faith leaders. They can remind you of why you started, help you see how far you have come, and pray or offer guidance. Reading faith-based stories of perseverance can also feed your spirit. You see how others overcame huge odds by trusting God and refusing to give up.

Take a Strategic Pause

Sometimes, the best way to persevere is to take a short break. If you are burned out, stepping away for a day or two can refill your mental and emotional well. Use this time to rest, pray, or do a fun activity. Then return with fresh eyes. A pause is different from quitting; it is more like pulling over to the side of the road to check the map and stretch your legs before continuing the journey.

Revisit Your Original Vision

Ask yourself, "Why did I start this project in the first place?" Maybe you had a passion to solve a problem or a calling to serve a certain group of people. Write that reason down and place it where you can see it daily. A strong sense of purpose can reignite your will to press on.

I nearly shut down my first business after six months. Sales were too slow, and I felt like I was letting my family down. Then, I prayed for clarity and remembered a moment when a customer told me my work changed her life. That memory became my lifeline. I pinned her thank-you note to my desk, reminding me that my mission mattered. It gave me the push to keep going another week, another month, and eventually, that business found stable ground.

Handling Discouragement, Criticism, and Comparison

Discouragement

It is natural to feel discouraged when results come slowly. You might think, "I am putting in so much effort, but nothing is happening." Yet many big results hide below the surface, like seeds growing roots before they sprout. In times of discouragement:

- **Focus on Small Wins:** Identify tiny steps you have accomplished, such as learning a new skill or helping a single customer.

- **Vent to a Safe Person:** Talking honestly with a friend or mentor can release built-up stress.
- **Pray for Renewed Strength:** Ask God to help you see progress you might be missing.

Criticism

When you step out and do something new, critics often show up. They may doubt your ideas or even belittle your efforts. It hurts, but not all criticism is bad. Sometimes, it reveals areas you can improve. Other times, it is just negativity you should not take to heart.

Ask If It Is Constructive: If there is truth in the feedback, use it to grow. If not, let it go and trust that not everyone will understand your calling.

Stay Calm: Responding to criticism with anger usually makes things worse. Instead, thank the person for sharing their view and move on if you must.

Comparison

It is easy to look at someone else's success and feel like you are behind. Yet everyone's path is different. What looks like instant success for them might be the result of years of hidden work. Comparing yourself to others often breeds envy or despair.

Focus on Your Own Race: **Keep your eyes on the steps you need to take,** not someone else's victory lap.

Celebrate Others' Wins: When you cheer for their achievements, you build a more positive mindset.

Pray for Contentment: Ask God to help you find peace in your own journey, trusting that your timing is unique.

One time, I spent hours scrolling through social media, watching a fellow entrepreneur who seemed to have it all. I felt crushed, wondering why my path was slower. Then, I met her in person and learned she had faced serious setbacks that she rarely mentioned online. Knowing her full story humbled me and helped me see that comparison can be misleading. Each of us has different rhythms and challenges along the way.

Building a Circle of Support for the Long Haul

Why You Need Other People

Consistency and perseverance become easier when you have friends or mentors cheering you on. Even the strongest individuals can crumble under pressure without a supportive community. Your circle of support can be family, like-minded business owners, faith-based small groups, or even an online community that shares your interests and values.

The Power of Accountability

When someone else knows your goals, you are more likely to stick to them. An accountability partner can check in on you weekly, asking if you completed the tasks you promised. Just knowing you have to give an update can motivate you on days you would rather procrastinate.

- Choose Wisely: Pick someone who is positive, honest, and genuinely cares about your success.
- Make It Regular: Set a specific time—like every Monday morning—to share progress and discuss challenges.

Mentors and Role Models

Mentors have already walked a similar path. They can warn you about common pitfalls and encourage you when you hit roadblocks. Role models inspire you from afar—maybe you read their books or follow their blog. Their stories of overcoming fear or failure can spark your own perseverance.

Be Proactive in Seeking Help: If you admire someone's journey, politely reach out and ask if they can offer occasional advice or if they recommend resources.

Add Faith Leaders to Your Network: If you are part of a church or faith community, talk to a pastor, priest, or spiritual mentor. They can offer prayer support and spiritual counsel.

I once joined a small entrepreneurial prayer group. We met every Friday morning, discussed our goals, and prayed for each other's businesses. We shared wins, but we also shared struggles. Knowing six other people were rooting for me gave me courage to try new ideas and to wake up and try again harder. Their feedback improved my projects. When I faced discouragement, they reminded me I was not alone. That circle of support often made the difference between quitting and pressing on.

Real-Life Stories of Consistency and Perseverance

The Cafe Owner Who Kept Showing Up

I know a cafe owner named Elise. For the first six months, her cafe saw more empty chairs than customers. She could have closed down, but each morning she faithfully unlocked the doors, greeted the few regulars who came, and tried small improvements—like a new pastry recipe or cheerful decorations. Gradually, word spread about her welcoming space and tasty treats. By the end of the first year, her cafe bustled with customers, many of whom admired her warmth and consistency. Elise says, "You never know which day will bring the breakthrough, so you show up every day."

The Dad Who Balanced Work and Study

A father of two small children dreamed of earning a college degree online. But he worked full-time, so he had to study late at night. Week after week, he did his coursework while the kids slept. He prayed for energy when he felt tired and asked God to help him balance his family time. Each morning, he woke up early to do any leftover reading. It took him longer than average students, but he eventually finished. He said, "It was tough, but doing a little bit each day got me across the finish line."

The Nonprofit Leader Who Faced Rejection

A nonprofit leader applied for grant after grant to fund a community project. Over and over, she got polite "no thank you" responses. She felt tempted to say, "This will never work." But her passion to help local families drove her to keep trying. She prayed for guidance, refined her proposals, and asked mentors for advice. After dozens of rejections, she finally got one "yes." That first "yes" opened more doors, and her project became a model for other towns. "If I had quit after the tenth or even the twentieth no," she said, "I would have missed the one yes that changed everything."

These stories remind us that success often hides behind long periods of faithful effort. If you keep showing up, keep refining your approach, and trust that your labor is not in vain, you might be closer to victory than you imagine. Don't let your mind wounder and get the best of you. Even when all signs say "no" continue moving on strong and most importantly – keep your faith.

My Own Experience—Sticking to a Vision

I want to share a more personal story about consistency and perseverance. A few years ago, I felt called to create a training course for people wanting to start small businesses. The idea excited me, but once I started, I realized how much work it took—outlining lessons, filming videos, building a website, and marketing it. Halfway through, I faced exhaustion. I also doubted if anyone would even buy the course.

At that point, I was tempted to shelve the project. Yet, each time I prayed, I felt a small inner voice say, "Finish what you started. Someone out there needs this." So I set a schedule: I worked one hour each weekday on the course content. Some days, I only managed 30 minutes because of family issues or a busy client load. But I refused to let a week pass without progress. Over months, the modules took shape. I also wrote a short daily devotion for myself to keep my mindset positive.

Finally, launch day arrived. Sales were not amazing, but a handful of people enrolled. Their feedback touched me deeply—one said it gave her the step-by-step guide she always needed. Encouraged, I kept improving the course, and eventually, it reached hundreds of students. Reflecting on that journey, I see it as a real-life example of how small, consistent steps and a spirit of perseverance—supported by faith—can turn a dream into reality.

Your Long March to Victory

Life does not usually offer shortcuts to meaningful success. The road can be winding, with moments of boredom and times of sheer frustration. Yet, consistency and perseverance act like your steady companions, ensuring that you keep inching forward, even when the finish line seems out of sight. Each day you show up, each time you refuse to quit, you build inner strength and move closer to your goal.

Remember:

Consistency is doing the right tasks again and again, forming habits that carry you through the ups and downs.

Perseverance is the resolve to keep going when obstacles stand in your way or when excitement fades.

Faith provides a powerful motivation to stay true to your purpose. By praying, reflecting, and trusting that your journey has meaning, you find the fuel to push past discouragement.

Small actions add up. A simple routine can lead to amazing results over time, much like a tiny seed grows into a large tree.

Lean on community. We are not meant to travel alone. Seek out mentors, friends, or groups who will cheer you on and hold you accountable.

If you are feeling stuck or weary right now, take heart. Revisit why you started, say a prayer for fresh determination, and tackle a small step today. Even if it is just organizing your workspace or making one important phone call, do it. Then, do another small step tomorrow.

Faith does not eliminate the long journey, but it gives you courage for each mile, confident that your steady beat will eventually create a beautiful song.

May you walk in the knowledge that your efforts matter, and that each day of consistency brings you closer to the harvest you have been working for. Keep going, trust the process, and let your perseverance write a story of triumph for others to see. When the results finally bloom, you will be able to say, "I stayed the course, and it was all worth it."

PART IV

ETHICS, SERVICE, AND AUTHENTIC LEADERSHIP

09

BUILDING AN ETHICAL BUSINESS

"Better is a little with righteousness than great revenues with injustice."

(PROVERBS 16:8)

Leading with Integrity

Imagine you walk into a store where the owner greets you with a warm smile, answers your questions honestly, and truly cares about your needs. The store might be small and simple, but something about it feels good. You trust the owner. You feel at ease. You want to come back, even if there are cheaper options elsewhere. That is the power of running an ethical business—people sense they are safe in your hands, and they respect you for it.

Building an ethical business means doing the right thing, even if it costs you more time, money, or effort. It means choosing honesty when it might be simpler to hide the truth. It means being fair to your customers, employees, and partners. You do not always chase the fastest way to earn cash; you choose what lines up with your beliefs and values. This might sound tough, especially in a world where shortcuts and tricks can appear tempting. But there is a deeper reward waiting for those who stand firm in their morals.

When you let ethics guide your business, you also let faith or higher principles shape your decisions. You see your work as more than just trading goods for money. You see it as a chance to serve, to shine a light in your field, and to leave a positive mark on the world. You believe that your actions matter beyond just the bottom line. Of course, you still want profits—business is about earning income. Yet, you do not sacrifice people or principles for a quick buck. Instead, you look for ways to bring true value into people's lives while staying true to your moral code.

In this chapter, you will learn how to build an ethical business that stands on strong values. You will see how faith can guide you in making choices that honor both your customers and the greater good. You will also explore practical steps you can take—from creating fair policies to treating your team well. By the end, you will have a clearer idea of how to merge faith-driven ethics with day-to-day operations. Whether your business is just a tiny seedling or already blooming, an ethical approach can help it flourish in ways that truly matter.

Why Ethics Matter in Business

A Foundation of Trust

Trust is a precious thing in business. When people trust you, they give you their time, money, and sometimes personal information. They believe you will not cheat or harm them. Ethical choices build this trust. If you keep your word about product quality, pricing, or deadlines, your customers and partners start to feel safe with you. Over time, this can lead to loyalty. They might return again and again because they feel respected. Trust, once gained, forms the backbone of your reputation.

Attracting and Keeping Customers

Have you ever heard a friend rave about a business that went "above and beyond"? Maybe the staff replaced a faulty product without hassle, or they kindly offered a discount because of a small inconvenience. Acts like these stand out. They show you care about the customer's experience more than just taking their money. Word spreads fast about businesses that treat people with fairness and respect.

People prefer to buy from companies they believe have good values. So, by being ethical, you can actually stand out in a crowded market.

Long-Term Success Over Short-Term Gains

An unethical company might see quick profits at first—like tricking people into high prices or hiding flaws in a product—but these tactics often lead to disaster over time. Once customers learn about shady methods, they leave and warn others. Lawsuits might follow. Your reputation gets stained, and rebuilding trust becomes very hard. Ethical business practices, on the other hand, aim for steady growth. They might move slower, but they build a strong house on a solid foundation. When hard times come, that solid moral core can keep you from collapsing.

Faith and Ethics—A Powerful Combination

Using Spiritual Values as a Compass

If you follow a faith tradition, you likely hold certain values—such as honesty, kindness, generosity, and respect for others. These values do not have to stay locked away in your personal life. They can guide your business decisions too. Imagine each time you face a tough call—like how much to charge a struggling client, or what to do if you accidentally overbilled someone—you pause and ask, "Which choice lines up with my spiritual beliefs?" This approach can give you clarity. You do not just guess or copy what the market does; you let deeper principles steer the wheel.

Finding Purpose Beyond Profit

Many faiths teach that life is about more than just making money. Yes, you need to pay bills and support your family. However, building an ethical business can also let you serve a higher calling. You might feel led to help your neighborhood by providing jobs or offering services that make people's lives better. You might choose to donate a portion of your earnings to charitable causes. When you run your company with a sense of divine purpose, you experience more fulfillment. Work turns into a mission, not just a grind.

Overcoming Temptations with Faith

Temptations often arise in the world of business—temptations to inflate numbers, break promises, or be sneaky with contracts. Faith can act like a sturdy fence around your heart. It reminds you that certain lines cannot be crossed. If you ever waver, prayer or spiritual reflection can bring you back, helping you see that a quick trick for short-term gain might harm your soul and your future. You trust that doing right, even when it is hard, will bring blessings in ways you might not see right away.

Common Ethical Dilemmas (and How to Handle Them)

Pricing and Transparency

Setting prices is tricky. You want a healthy profit, but you do not want to rip anyone off. Some businesses hide extra fees or inflate prices way beyond fair market value. An ethical approach is to be open about costs. If you believe your service or product is worth a certain amount, explain why. Show the value, the quality, and the care that goes into it. If a price is high, stand by it honestly rather than using sneaky tactics to trick people into paying more than they should.

> *Tip: Offer clear quotes or invoices. Break down the costs if possible. People appreciate knowing exactly what they are paying for.*

Advertising and Marketing

Have you ever seen an ad that promised the moon but delivered a cheap knockoff? Ethical marketing focuses on telling the truth in a persuasive way. You can highlight the benefits of your offer without lying or overselling. If something has a limitation, do not hide it—make sure the customer understands. If your product is not suitable for certain people, let them know. Honesty in marketing might seem risky, but it often creates loyal fans who trust you more over time.

Tip: If you use testimonials, make sure they are real. Do not make up glowing reviews. This might boost sales in the short run, but it breaks trust once people find out.

Employee Treatment

Your staff members are not just workers; they are people with dreams, families, and personal struggles. Ethical business owners treat employees fairly, paying them decent wages and showing respect. This might mean giving them a safe work environment, listening to their concerns, or offering growth opportunities. Avoid exploitation—overworking people without proper pay or benefits can harm morale. When employees feel valued, they often show more loyalty and do better work.

Tip: Encourage open communication. If something is wrong in the workplace, let employees speak up without fear of punishment. Solve problems together.

Handling Competitors

Competition can bring out the best or the worst in people. Some might spy on rivals, spread false rumors, or sabotage them. An ethical stance means focusing on your own excellence. Do not tear others down; build yourself up by improving your products or services. Speak honestly about what you offer without lying about what competitors do. You can be tough in business without being cruel or dishonest.

Tip: In some cases, you can even cooperate with competitors if it benefits both sides. Collaboration might open new doors and show clients you are confident in your own strengths.

Setting a Moral Code for Your Business

Crafting a Guiding Statement

Your moral code is like a compass that points to True North. It should reflect your core values and the principles you refuse to compromise on. Try writing a short statement that sums up these ethics. For example: "We promise honesty, fairness, and respect in all dealings. We vow never to lie to or mislead our customers or employees." Keep this statement visible—on your website, in your office, or even in staff training manuals.

Aligning Policies and Procedures

Words matter, but actions speak louder. Once you have a moral code, create policies and procedures that line up with it. For instance, if you value transparency, set rules about open communication with customers and staff. Decide how you will handle returns, complaints, or conflicts. Make sure these rules are fair and consistent, showing you mean what you say about ethics.

Communicating the Code

Share your moral code with everyone in your organization. Teach new hires about it. Remind long-time workers as well. This does not have to be boring. You could hold a short workshop where people discuss real-life situations and how to solve them ethically. Encouraging staff to suggest improvements to the code can keep it relevant. The more people feel involved, the stronger the commitment to these values becomes.

Creating an Ethical Culture with Employees

Leading by Example

As the leader or owner, you set the tone. If you treat people kindly and fairly, your employees will likely do the same. If they see you cutting corners or lying to suppliers, they might think it is acceptable.

Leadership by example is one of the most powerful ways to ensure an ethical culture. You show, not just tell, how to act with integrity.

Fair Wages and Benefits

Money matters in business, but it should not be the only factor. Paying people a just wage shows them you respect their time and energy. If possible, offer benefits like healthcare or flexible hours that help them balance work and family. While you have to manage costs, investing in your team often yields higher morale and loyalty. They will likely stay longer, saving you from the costs of high turnover.

Open Communication and Conflict Resolution

An ethical workplace invites employees to share ideas and speak up about problems. Encourage open-door policies where a worker can talk to you or a manager without fear. When conflicts arise—maybe someone feels unfairly treated—address them quickly and fairly. Hear both sides, seek the truth, and find a solution that respects all parties if possible. A workplace that ignores or hides conflicts can breed resentment and dishonesty.

Celebrating Good Deeds

Rewarding employees who show ethical behavior can reinforce your culture. Maybe someone went the extra mile to help a struggling customer, or they reported a safety issue that could have harmed co-workers. Shine a light on these positive acts. Let the team see that good morals are noticed and valued. Small awards, public acknowledgments, or simple thank-you notes can make a big difference.

Ethical Marketing and Sales Strategies

Being Clear About What You Offer

When you market your goods or services, present them truthfully. Show real photos, list actual features, and avoid exaggerating results. If your product has limits—like only working in certain climates—make that known. A disappointed buyer who feels misled might leave negative reviews or never return. But a buyer who knows exactly what they are getting will often appreciate the honesty, even if the product is not perfect for everyone.

Respecting Customer Privacy

Data protection is crucial in today's digital world. If you collect emails, phone numbers, or personal details, safeguard them. Do not sell them to third parties without permission or bombard people with spam. Let customers know how you store and use their information. Show them that you value their trust. This approach not only meets legal requirements but also reflects care and respect.

Avoiding High-Pressure Tactics

Some salespeople push so hard that customers feel trapped. They might guilt someone into a purchase or make false "limited-time" claims. While you might close a few quick deals this way, you risk creating resentment. Ethical sales aim to match the right product with the right person. You focus on understanding their needs and seeing if your solution truly fits. If it does not, have the courage to say so. People often respect a salesperson who is honest enough to admit, "This might not be the best option for you."

Giving Back to the Community

One powerful marketing approach is to let customers see how your business supports a greater good. Maybe you donate a portion of sales to a local shelter, or your employees volunteer once a month. Share these stories genuinely, not as a brag but as a way to show you care about more than profit. Customers may be glad to support a business that contributes to the welfare of the community.

Handling Tough Decisions and Mistakes

When Conflicts Arise

In business, conflicts are sure to happen—maybe a supplier fails to deliver on time, or a client feels you did not meet expectations. You might feel tempted to deny blame or shift it to someone else. But an ethical stance says you handle the issue head-on. First, gather the facts. Then, if you are at fault, own up to it. Offer a plan to fix it. This might mean a refund, an apology, or a changed policy to prevent future issues. Owning mistakes can feel scary, but it builds immense respect and trust.

Balancing Profits and Principles

You might face a time when sticking to your ethics seems to cost you a lot of money. For example, an investor offers a huge sum, but wants you to cut corners on safety or mislead customers about product features. Or maybe a client wants you to hide some facts so they can pay less tax. Saying "no" to unethical deals can hurt financially in the short run. Yet, it can save you from bigger losses later, not to mention keeping your conscience clear. Faith can help you stand firm, reminding you that God honors integrity in the end.

Learning from Failure

Sometimes, you will fail ethically. You might lose your temper with a worker or stretch the truth to close a sale. Or you may discover a small dishonest act you overlooked. When this happens, do not spiral into shame or give up on trying to be ethical. Recognize the slip, correct it, and learn. Apologize if needed. Then strengthen your moral safeguards so you do not repeat the same error. This humble approach often brings growth, showing others that you hold yourself accountable to high standards.

The Blessings (and Challenges) of Ethical Leadership

Earning Deep Respect

When you run your business with integrity, people take notice. Customers become loyal. Employees stick around and speak well of you. Community members see you as a reliable presence. This kind of respect is not something you can buy—it is earned by day-to-day moral choices. Over time, your positive reputation can open doors to partnerships or bigger opportunities. People want to work with someone they trust.

Facing Criticism

Interestingly, some might criticize or mock you for being "too nice" or "too honest." They might say you are leaving money on the table or not being ambitious enough. Your faith-based approach could confuse those who only chase profits. This is part of the challenge of ethics. You can stand out in ways that not everyone understands or likes. However, staying true to your core keeps you stable, even when critics grumble. Plus, there are likely many silent admirers who see your courage and applaud you quietly.

Greater Inner Peace

Knowing you are doing right, even behind closed doors, can bring deep inner peace. You sleep better, free from the worry that someone will expose a lie or shady deal. You can look your employees and customers in the eye without guilt. This peace is priceless. It might not show on a financial statement, but it affects how you approach every part of your life. You no longer carry a burden of secrets or fear that unethical choices could crumble your foundation.

Real-Life Stories of Ethical Businesses

The Honest Mechanic

In one town, a mechanic became famous for his straightforward approach. If a customer came in with a small problem, he would fix it quickly and charge a fair rate—sometimes, even less than they expected. He did not upsell unneeded parts or trick people who knew little about cars. Word spread that he was the most honest mechanic in town. He might not have become a millionaire, but he gained steady work and respect. Locals said, "You can trust him with your eyes closed." Such is the power of consistent honesty.

The Fair-Fashion Brand

A small clothing brand decided to pay their factory workers a living wage, even though it cut into profits. They also used environmentally friendly materials. Their price tags were higher than fast-fashion stores, but they explained the reasons clearly to customers. Over time, they found a loyal fan base who valued ethical production. Though they started small, they grew a reputation as a company that cared about people and the planet. Their faith in doing right led them to share updates on worker benefits and show real photos of the factories. Customers felt proud to wear clothes made with integrity.

The Grocery Store That Gave Away Surplus

A local grocery store manager hated seeing leftover produce go to waste. He teamed up with a local food bank, donating near-expired but still safe food to help feed needy families. Some people said, "You could sell that for a discount." But the store felt called to help the hungry. This act of generosity did not ruin their business—in fact, it improved their image. People heard about the donations and wanted to support the store. This story shows that compassion can blend with commerce in a beautiful way.

Personal Testimony—My Own Lessons in Ethical Practice

I want to share a personal story of when I faced an ethical crossroad. Early in my career, I joined a small team launching a new product. Our leader suggested we hide certain flaws in the product's design so we could hit the market sooner. I felt uneasy. If we sold it as-is, people might have a bad experience and lose money. But I also feared speaking up and rocking the boat. I prayed about it and decided that my conscience would not let me stay silent.

I approached the leader privately, explaining my concerns. At first, he was annoyed. He said time was ticking, and we would lose potential profits if we delayed. But I kept calm, suggesting we be honest about the product's limitations. I also offered ideas for quick fixes that might help. In the end, we did decide to disclose the known issues. We spent a bit more time ironing out major bugs before launching. Our release was a little late, but we had fewer refunds and negative reviews. In the long run, that honesty saved our brand's reputation. It also taught me that doing right might be inconvenient, but it can prevent bigger headaches later.

Now, whenever I am tempted to cut corners, I remember that moment. It was scary to speak up, but the relief I felt afterward was priceless. I also saw how God provided a better outcome than I expected. Rather than losing everything by slowing down, we gained a stronger foundation to build upon. That experience reminded me that faith and ethics walk together, giving you courage to stand firm when others might yield to pressure.

Embracing the Ethical Path for Lasting Impact

Building an ethical business is not just a "nice idea"—it is a path that can guide you through all kinds of challenges and opportunities. When you center your decisions on honesty, respect, and service, you lay down strong roots. You attract customers who admire your integrity, employees who trust your leadership, and partners who value your sincerity. Even if the road feels longer or more difficult at times, the rewards can be far greater and more lasting.

By mixing faith with ethics, you tap into a deeper purpose. You see yourself not just as a seller of goods but as someone who can make lives better. You see your work as an expression of spiritual values, a form of service that pleases God and enriches your community. Yes, you might face critics who think you are missing out on quick profits. Yes, you might have to turn down deals that clash with your morals. But you also gain peace of mind, a shining reputation, and a sense of fulfillment money cannot buy.

As you walk this ethical path, remember to keep learning. Update your policies, refine your moral code, and keep listening to your conscience and your faith. Talk with mentors, share stories with like-minded people, and remain open to new ways of living out your values in the marketplace. Whether you run a tiny online shop or a large company, the principles remain the same: treat people with respect, be honest, create real value, and honor your deepest beliefs. In doing so, you build a business that can stand the test of time and bring genuine good into the world—one ethical choice at a time.

10

LEADERSHIP THROUGH SERVING OTHERS

"Whoever desires to become great among you, let him be your servant."

(MATTHEW 20:26)

The Heart of True Leadership

When you think of a leader, you might picture someone standing at the top of a tall ladder, giving orders to the people below. Yet, there is another kind of leadership—one that does not shine from above, but instead meets people at eye level, helping them grow and thrive. This is called servant leadership: leading by serving others. Rather than barking commands, you build trust, show respect, and look out for the needs of those around you.

Servant leadership is not a new idea. It has roots in many faith traditions and appears in the stories of great leaders throughout history. You find this spirit in the people who roll up their sleeves and work alongside their teams, who pay attention to each person's struggles, and who celebrate success as a shared victory. They do not view themselves as more important than anyone else, even if they hold a high position. Instead, they see leadership as a calling to serve.

In business, leading through serving others may sound risky at first. "Shouldn't the boss be in charge?" you might wonder. But servant leaders know that by lifting up their team, they actually create a stronger, healthier workplace. They discover that when people feel valued, they give their best effort. Customers notice the difference, too. A team that cares for each other often cares more for the customers, creating a ripple effect of kindness and quality that benefits the whole organization.

In this chapter, you will learn how servant leadership works in practice and how it can shape your business for the better. You will explore ways to mentor your team, help them grow their skills, and foster a culture of respect and collaboration. You will also see how faith can guide you to put others first without losing sight of your goals. By the end, you will understand that leadership is not about you standing on top; it is about supporting others, so you all rise together.

What Is Servant Leadership?

Serving as a Way of Leading

Servant leadership flips the usual leadership model upside down. Instead of a traditional pyramid where the leader sits at the top, you picture the leader at the bottom, upholding the team. Your role is to support and empower rather than to dominate or control. You still make decisions and set goals, but you do so with the team's well-being in mind. You consider questions like, "How will this choice help my employees grow?" or "Will it nurture a better future for those who depend on me?"

Why Putting People First Works

When you serve your team, you build a foundation of trust. People see you genuinely care about their concerns—whether it is a heavy workload, a new skill they want to learn, or a personal challenge. By addressing these needs, you create loyalty and motivation. Your team members stop feeling like cogs in a machine and start feeling like valued contributors. This sense of belonging leads to higher engagement and creativity. In other words, people tend to do their best work when they feel respected and safe.

Biblical and Historical Roots

Many faith traditions highlight the idea of a leader who serves. In Christianity, for example, Jesus washed His disciples' feet, showing that true leaders are not above humble tasks. Historical figures like Mahatma Gandhi or Mother Teresa also demonstrated leadership by caring for the poor and vulnerable. Their influence came not from shouting or demanding power, but from their willingness to serve. By following these examples, you draw on a deep well of wisdom about what it means to guide others with compassion and vision.

The Core Principles of Servant Leadership

Listening and Understanding

One of the first steps in serving your team is to listen—really listen—to what they have to say. This goes beyond nodding politely; it involves asking questions and letting people speak without fear of judgment. Listening shows respect and helps you learn what your team truly needs. You might discover that a shy employee wants more chances to practice public speaking, or that a veteran worker struggles with new technology. Once you understand, you can offer tailored support.

Practical Tip: Schedule regular one-on-one talks with each team member. Ask open-ended questions like, "How can I help make your job easier?" or "What is one thing you wish we did differently?" Then, follow through on their suggestions whenever possible.

Empathy and Compassion

Empathy means stepping into someone else's shoes and feeling what they feel. You do not have to solve all their problems, but you show that you care. When an employee faces a family crisis, for example, a servant leader might offer flexible hours or find a coworker who can assist with their tasks. Or if someone is discouraged by a tough project, you remind them they are not alone. By treating people kindly in their low moments, you gain their trust and respect.

Practical Tip: Keep an eye out for signs of stress. If you see someone struggling, gently ask, "Is everything okay? How can I support you right now?" A few kind words can mean the world to someone under pressure.

Nurturing Growth

Servant leaders do not just assign work; they help people develop their talents and discover new strengths. You might provide extra training for someone who wants to sharpen a skill or let a junior employee shadow you in meetings to learn the ropes. By investing in their growth, you signal that you believe in their potential, which boosts confidence and drives better performance.

Practical Tip: Set aside a small budget or time for professional development. This could be paying for online courses, inviting a speaker to share knowledge, or creating a mentorship program. Let employees know you value their personal and professional advancement.

Humility

Humility does not mean you lack confidence. It means recognizing you do not have all the answers and that your role is to lift others, not overshadow them. You admit mistakes when you make them, rather than blaming the team or hiding errors. You also celebrate others' successes without hogging the spotlight. Humility helps keep ego from blocking true collaboration.

Practical Tip: When a project goes well, publicly thank those who contributed. Point out their specific efforts. This spreads the credit around, encouraging everyone to keep pushing for excellence.

Faith as a Guiding Force

Letting Spiritual Values Shape Your Leadership

If you follow a faith tradition, you have a set of values—like kindness, honesty, and compassion. These values become a guiding star for how you treat your employees and customers. You see them not just as business assets, but as people with unique gifts and dreams. Faith can nudge you to think beyond short-term profits. You ask, "How does this decision affect my team's well-being?" or "Am I being fair and truthful, as my beliefs teach me to be?"

Personal Example: I once struggled with how to discipline an employee who kept missing deadlines. My gut reaction was anger—I wanted to give a harsh warning. But I recalled the value of patience taught in my faith. I took a breath, prayed for wisdom, and then sat down with the employee. I found out she was caring for an ill parent, which caused her lateness. We worked out a plan for flexible hours and a new task schedule. The result was a more engaged worker who felt valued, and she eventually caught up with her deadlines.

Leading with a Servant Heart

In many religious teachings, leadership is framed as a sacred responsibility. You are entrusted with caring for and guiding others. This mindset can turn daily tasks—like assigning projects or planning budgets—into acts of service. You want to succeed, but not at the cost of neglecting your team's dignity or health. Instead, you lean on your faith to remind you that every person matters.

Prayer, Reflection, and Guidance

In moments of tough decisions—like layoffs, mergers, or conflicts between team members—you can pause for prayer or quiet reflection. This helps you step back and ask: "What is the loving, fair, or just thing to do here?" While you might not receive a direct voice from above, you often gain a clearer sense of what aligns with your moral and spiritual compass. This approach can make even the hardest choices more manageable, knowing you have tried to remain faithful to your calling as a servant leader.

Practical Ways to Serve Your Team

Mentoring and Coaching

Leaders who serve invest time in coaching. Maybe you hold quick weekly check-ins with each employee to discuss challenges or goals. You offer tips, resources, or connections that help them move forward. By sharing your expertise and genuinely wanting them to grow, you show care. Mentoring also helps you spot future leaders within your organization—people who can later take on bigger responsibilities.

Implementation Idea: If you run a larger team, set up a buddy system where new hires pair with seasoned workers for the first few months. This helps newcomers feel welcomed and supported.

Sharing Responsibility

Servant leadership is not about doing everything yourself. It is about equipping your team so they can step up. You assign tasks that stretch their skills, allowing them to gain confidence. When you trust someone with an important duty, it sends the message, "I believe in you." Be available if they stumble, but do not hover. Let them learn. This approach fosters a sense of ownership across the team.

Implementation Idea: Rotate the role of "meeting facilitator" among team members. Each week, a different person leads the discussion and sets the agenda. This helps everyone develop leadership and communication skills.

Encouraging Collaboration

A leader who serves others sees teamwork as vital. You break down silos (areas that are cut off from each other) and push people to share information and help each other. Maybe you set up regular brainstorming sessions or cross-department projects. If employees see that you value cooperation, they are more likely to work together, preventing power struggles or competition that harms the group.

Implementation Idea: Start a weekly "huddle" where people quickly update each other on projects. Encourage them to ask if anyone needs help. Celebrate small wins. Over time, these huddles build a culture of unity.

Recognizing Individual Strengths

Everyone has unique strengths—some excel at creative thinking, others at organization, and still others at empathy or detail work. As a servant leader, you observe these strengths and shape tasks or roles that let them shine. When people use their natural talents, they are happier and more productive. They feel seen and appreciated.

Implementation Idea: Use simple personality or strength assessments (like StrengthsFinder or DISC) to learn your team's preferred styles. Then, give tasks that play to those strengths, or pair people whose skills complement each other.

Serving Customers by Serving Your Team

The Ripple Effect

When employees feel valued and supported, they tend to give better service to customers. They are not just following rigid scripts; they genuinely want to help. A positive environment behind the scenes often shows up front, in how team members speak to and assist clients. By serving your team well, you indirectly serve your customers. It is like watering the roots of a plant and watching the flowers bloom.

Empowering Employees to Help Customers

In some businesses, employees must follow strict rules that can leave customers frustrated. A servant leader looks for ways to give their workers freedom to solve problems. If a customer has a complaint, for example, you allow your team to address it quickly, even if it means offering a small discount or a replacement item. This trust empowers employees to act in the moment, leading to happier customers and faster solutions.

> *Practical Tip: Set guidelines rather than rigid scripts. Tell employees, "You can offer up to X dollars in a discount if a customer is upset," or "Feel free to swap a product if you see it is defective." Let them use judgment within those boundaries.*

Being a Role Model for Customer Care

As the leader, you set the tone for how customers should be treated. If you show empathy during a tough customer call or personally reach out to resolve a conflict, your team sees that standard. They learn that each customer is not just a transaction, but a person you want to serve well. This attitude can become contagious throughout the organization, creating a reputation for outstanding service that draws people in.

> *Personal Example: Once, a furious customer called about a botched delivery. I could have handed it off to a lower-level staffer. Instead, I listened to the complaint, apologized sincerely, and offered a prompt solution. My employees noticed. Later, they told me it made them realize we truly care, and they began to handle calls with the same patience and concern.*

Overcoming Challenges in Servant Leadership

Balancing Service and Authority

Being a servant leader does not mean letting everyone walk over you. You still have to set rules, meet deadlines, and hold people accountable. The key is doing so with respect and clarity. You explain why a rule exists, invite input, and stay fair. If someone repeatedly breaks policies or underperforms, you address it firmly, but without demeaning them. Servant leadership mixes kindness with responsibility.

> *Practical Tip: Use a performance review system that focuses on both results and behavior. If someone is not meeting standards, discuss ways to improve, but also be ready to enforce consequences if they refuse to change.*

Handling Criticism

When you try to serve others, some might doubt your motives or see it as weakness. They might say, "You are too soft" or "This is not how business works." Criticism can sting, especially if it comes from friends or mentors you respect. However, stand firm. Servant leadership is not about people-pleasing. It is about following your principles and nurturing a healthy environment. Over time, the results often speak for themselves.

> *Advice: Use prayer or personal reflection when criticism hits. Ask, "Is there any truth in this feedback?" If yes, adjust. If not, remain confident in your approach.*

Avoiding Burnout

Serving others can be fulfilling but also draining if you do not practice self-care. You might try to solve everyone's issues, leaving little time for your own tasks or rest. Remember: a tired, frustrated leader cannot effectively serve anyone. Take breaks, delegate duties, and keep your own spiritual and emotional health in check. Healthy boundaries do not make you selfish; they keep you strong enough to keep helping.

Practical Tip: Schedule "quiet hours" for yourself each week—no meetings, calls, or emails. Use that time for personal tasks, learning, or prayer. Encourage your team to do the same, so everyone respects each other's downtime.

Real-Life Examples of Servant Leadership

The Boss Who Was Always Available

In one small company, the owner had a simple rule: my door is always open. She encouraged employees to drop by with any concern or idea. She listened attentively, asked questions, and made changes when she could. Over time, people felt more willing to share both their struggles and creative solutions. The business thrived, partly because no big problem stayed hidden for long. The owner's availability served the team's needs and built a family-like atmosphere.

A Team That Cared for the Community

A medium-sized retail store decided to reflect the servant-leader mindset by helping its local neighborhood. Employees, led by their manager, volunteered monthly at a nearby shelter, donating time and resources. Customers heard about these efforts and began to see the store as a community ally rather than just a place to shop. Profits rose, but more importantly, morale soared among employees who felt proud to work for a company that practiced caring leadership inside and outside the workplace.

The Restaurant Where Everyone Pitched In

In a bustling restaurant, the head chef was known to step out of the kitchen during busy hours to serve customers directly or help the waitstaff deliver dishes. When a dish came out late, he apologized to the table personally. When the dishwasher called in sick, he offered to help rinse plates. His example set a tone where everyone understood that no job was "too small" or "beneath" anyone. They worked as a true team, and customers frequently noticed the warm, cohesive atmosphere.

Personal Testimony—My Journey of Serving First

I remember the moment I realized that true leadership meant serving others rather than bossing them around. Years ago, I led a small project team that was struggling to meet deadlines. I was stressed and started snapping at people. I thought, "If I just push them harder, they will work faster." But it only caused resentment. Tensions rose, and mistakes multiplied.

One evening, I took time to pray, asking for guidance on how to turn things around. A quiet thought nudged me: serve your team. The next morning, instead of scolding them about delays, I asked each person what was blocking them. One said she lacked training on a certain software; another was juggling personal issues at home. I spent the next days finding training resources and adjusting workloads to suit each person's strengths. I also brought in coffee and donuts just to show appreciation.

At first, these acts felt small, almost silly. But morale improved. People felt heard and respected. The software expert finished tasks quicker, and the woman with home troubles got a more flexible schedule. Deadlines began to be met again. When the project wrapped up successfully, I realized it was not my authority that saved it—it was serving my team's needs that made the difference. That project shaped my leadership philosophy forever, teaching me that a servant's heart can steer a struggling group toward unity and success.

Steps to Grow as a Servant Leader

Examine Your Motives

Ask yourself why you want to lead. Is it for prestige or control? Or do you genuinely want to help people and achieve shared goals? If you find ego creeping in, use prayer or reflection to refocus on serving. This honesty will help you stay grounded.

Practice Daily Acts of Service

Small gestures add up. Greet your team by name each morning, help restock the office kitchen, or send a personal note to someone who did good work. These little moments show you are present and caring.

Encourage Feedback

Servant leaders welcome feedback—even if it is negative. Create safe spaces where your team can tell you what is not working. Listen with an open mind, avoid being defensive, and thank them for their honesty. Acting on their feedback proves you value their voices.

Keep Learning

Leadership evolves. Read books on servant leadership, attend workshops, or find a mentor whose style you admire. Stay curious about better ways to serve your team. Ask them for ideas on how you can improve. A leader who keeps growing inspires others to do the same.

Stay Connected to Faith

Continue feeding your spiritual life through prayer, scripture, or fellowship with fellow believers. This keeps your heart soft and your vision clear. In times of stress or confusion, return to your faith's core teachings about humility, kindness, and love for others. Let those teachings shape your choices.

Leading as a Servant, Creating Lasting Impact

Leading through serving others does not mean you abandon high standards or ignore profits. It means you recognize that people are at the heart of every success. When your team feels supported and inspired, they will put in their best efforts. Customers sense the genuine care in your workplace and respond with loyalty. Over time, your business grows not just in revenue, but in reputation and strong relationships.

True leadership is not about standing on a pedestal; it is about offering your hand to help others climb higher. By listening, empathizing, nurturing growth, and staying humble, you practice a style of leadership that can transform your work environment. Even if challenges arise—like tight deadlines or financial pressures—you tackle them together, guided by a spirit of service rather than fear or control.

As you continue your journey, remember how faith can deepen your commitment to servant leadership. You can view your role as a calling to reflect love, kindness, and integrity in all you do. Each decision becomes an opportunity to serve, to uplift, and to show the world that good business and good values can go hand in hand.

May you find joy in putting others first. May your team thrive under your compassionate guidance. And may your leadership ripple far beyond your own business, touching lives and inspiring others to embrace a more caring way of working. This is the power of serving first, of leading from the heart, and of honoring the greater good in every choice you make.

11

FAITH IN MARKETING AND OUTREACH

"Let your light so shine before men, that they may see your good works and glorify your Father in heaven."

(MATTHEW 5:16)

Sharing Your Light with the World

Picture a lighthouse standing on a cliff, shining its beam across dark waters. It offers guidance and safety to ships searching for the shore. In many ways, marketing and outreach work like that lighthouse. They help others see what you offer, guiding them toward a solution or service that can brighten their day. Yet, you do not want just any light—you want a light powered by your deepest values and guided by your faith.

When you blend faith with marketing and outreach, you shine in a unique way. You are not just saying, "Buy from me!" or "Pick our company!" You are sharing something deeper: your heart for serving, your hope to make lives better, and your trust that good can come from honest business practices. Marketing becomes more than promotion; it becomes a chance to connect with people, learn their needs, and let them see your genuine care.

At first, you might wonder how faith fits into advertising slogans or social media posts. Yet, faith can quietly shape everything you do—how you present your brand, how you speak about your mission, and how you treat customers. By weaving spiritual values into your outreach, you build a bridge of trust. Instead of feeling pushy or fake, your marketing feels honest and kind. People sense something different about you: a sincere warmth that sets you apart from companies chasing only profit.

In this chapter, you will learn practical ways to integrate faith into your marketing and outreach. You will discover how to tell your story, show compassion in your ads, and serve the community in ways that build genuine relationships. You will also see how prayer and reflection can guide your decisions, helping you stay faithful to your calling. By the end, you will have a roadmap for spreading the word about your business in a way that honors both your customers and your Creator. Let us begin by exploring what faith-driven marketing looks like and why it matters in our ever-busy world.

Defining Faith-Driven Marketing

Marketing with Heart

Most people think of marketing as a way to grab attention and sell products. Faith-driven marketing goes deeper. It focuses on the person behind each dollar spent. Instead of aiming for the sale alone, you aim to meet real needs. You are not just pushing a message; you are sharing hope and value. For instance, if you sell healthy snacks, you might highlight how your snacks help families eat better and feel good, rather than just saying, "Low price! Buy now!"

By connecting with people's deeper desires—like health, peace, or community—you build trust. Your marketing says, "I see you. I want to help," instead of, "I want your money." This approach might take longer to show results, but it often creates loyal fans who appreciate your sincerity.

Faith as Your Moral Compass

Faith-driven marketing also means you hold yourself to a higher standard of honesty and respect. You do not trick people with hidden fees or exaggerate your claims just to make a quick profit. If your product or service has a limitation, you say so clearly. You treat your audience as friends you care about, not targets you want to manipulate.

In many faith traditions, honesty and love guide how you speak to others. Bringing these values into marketing can mean choosing not to run ads that scare people into buying. Instead, you focus on ads that inspire or educate. Faith reminds you that while business is important, people matter even more. This mindset shapes every decision, from the words you write in a brochure to the tone of your social media posts.

Serving Over Selling

Faith-based entrepreneurs often see themselves as servants rather than salespeople. They ask, "How can I serve my customers?" They design products or services that solve real problems or bring genuine joy. Their marketing approach then flows from that mission of serving. They are not afraid to show compassion or generosity, like offering free samples, trial periods, or educational tips with no strings attached.

Yes, a business must make money, but the purpose is broader: to bless customers and even the community. When your heart is set on serving, you market with integrity. People sense your authenticity, and they want to learn more about what you do. Over time, that trust leads to strong relationships, repeated sales, and positive word-of-mouth that grows your reach.

Telling Your Story with Authenticity

Why Stories Matter

People love stories. Think about children who beg to hear a bedtime tale—even as adults, we crave narratives that speak to our hearts. When you share your story—why you started your business, what challenges you faced, and how faith helped you overcome them—you become relatable. Your audience sees a real person behind the brand, not just a cold logo or slogan.

This storytelling can happen in many places: on your website's "About Us" page, in blog posts, in videos, or even in simple social media captions. By tying your faith journey to your business, you show how your values shape your decisions. Customers who share your beliefs may be drawn to your honesty, while others might simply appreciate your openness and passion.

Personal Touch vs. Over-Sharing

While authenticity is key, it is wise to find a balance. You do not need to reveal every personal detail or turn your business account into your private journal. Instead, focus on moments that show how faith guided your path. For example, if you felt led to start a tutoring service after seeing kids struggle in your neighborhood, tell that story. Show how your faith sparked your desire to help.

As you share, keep your audience in mind. Some people might not share your spiritual beliefs, but they can still connect with your empathy, your perseverance, or your honest struggles. Make your story accessible to many kinds of people. Being genuine is about revealing your heart while still respecting the boundaries of your listeners.

Consistency in Your Brand Voice

Your brand voice is how your business "sounds" to others. If faith and caring are core parts of your story, let those elements shine consistently. That means using kind and uplifting language in your emails, ads, and social media replies. It means staying polite even if someone criticizes you online. Over time, people notice if your brand voice matches the compassionate story you tell. If there is a mismatch, trust erodes.

Building a consistent voice takes practice. You might create a small style guide for your team: a few simple principles like "We always respond with respect," "We admit our mistakes openly," and "We speak with hope, not fear." By following these guidelines, your outreach stays true to the faith-driven message at the heart of your business.

Reflecting Your Values in Your Marketing Materials

Choosing Inspiring Images and Messages

When preparing marketing materials—posters, flyers, social media graphics—your faith-inspired values can guide the look and feel. You might use bright, uplifting colors and images that show friendship, service, or kindness. If you run a healthcare clinic, for instance, you might feature real patients smiling, or staff members gently caring for someone. The pictures hint that you value compassion over hype.

In the words you choose, keep them honest and gentle. Avoid fear-based language that pressures people. Instead, highlight hope, benefits, and real-life outcomes. Suppose you sell home security devices. You might focus on the peace of mind families gain, rather than scaring them with dramatic crime stats. This angle aligns more with a caring, faith-centered perspective, showing your aim to protect rather than profit from fear.

Ethical Advertising

Faith-driven marketing avoids tricks that fool or manipulate. For example, do not show a super deluxe product in an ad if your actual item is simpler. If you say a service is "all-inclusive," but there are hidden fees, that is misleading. Even small exaggerations can harm trust. Let your conscience guide your claims, ensuring they hold up in reality.

Advertising also covers where and how you place your messages. Think twice about advertising on websites or platforms that clash with your moral values—such as websites hosting hateful content. It might cost more to be selective, but staying true to your principles matters more than easy ad spots. Remember: your ads reflect your brand. If they appear next to inappropriate or dishonest material, it can damage how people see you.

Faith-Inspired Colors, Symbols, and Themes?

Some faith-based businesses include subtle spiritual symbols or verses in their marketing. Others prefer to keep those details private, focusing on broader messages of love or service. There is no single right way. The main goal is alignment between your marketing and your heart. If a scripture verse on your brochure feels genuine and fits your brand, go for it. But if it feels forced, skip it. It is better to show your faith through actions and honest words than to paste religious symbols without real meaning behind them.

Building Relationships Through Community Outreach

Outreach as an Extension of Your Mission

Community outreach means going beyond your products to serve your town, city, or online community. Faith often inspires acts of kindness—like sponsoring a youth sports team, hosting a fundraising event for a local charity, or volunteering your skills. When people see you actually caring for others, they realize you are not just talking the talk. You are living your values.

Outreach can be as simple as offering free workshops about your area of expertise. If you run a bakery, maybe you teach a basic bread-making class for kids and parents. If you sell organic produce, perhaps you donate fresh items to a local food pantry. Through these acts, you meet people in real life, share knowledge, and brighten your corner of the world. The goodwill you create often results in natural word-of-mouth marketing, but that is just a bonus. The main reward is helping others.

Collaborating with Faith Communities

If your personal faith community wants to support local businesses, teaming up can be powerful. You might sponsor a booth at a church fair or provide snacks for a youth event. Alternatively, you can partner with multiple faith groups, bridging denominations or traditions to serve a larger cause—like a city cleanup or a back-to-school drive for children. In these moments, you become more than a company; you become part of a bigger tapestry of support and compassion.

Social Media Outreach with a Purpose

Many folks hang out online these days, so social media can be a place to live out your faith-based outreach. Instead of using social channels just to push sales, you can share uplifting stories, helpful tips, or encouraging words. If you find an inspiring quote that matches your message, post it with a short reflection. Invite your followers to share how they are practicing kindness in their neighborhood. Over time, your social media accounts become a source of hope rather than just another sales feed.

Prayer and Reflection in Marketing Decisions

Slowing Down Before Major Campaigns

Marketing often feels rushed. There is pressure to post daily, launch ads fast, and keep up with trends. But faith teaches the wisdom of pausing and seeking guidance. Before releasing a major campaign, take a moment to pray or reflect. Ask for clarity: "Am I presenting my product truthfully? Does this campaign respect my audience?" That brief pause can prevent costly mistakes or regret.

When you feel anxiety about competition or sales targets, turning to prayer can calm your heart. You remember that your worth does not depend on beating others, but on fulfilling your calling with integrity. This trust can give you a creative edge, too, since a peaceful mind often dreams up better ideas than a worried one.

Checking Motives

Faith-based marketing challenges you to examine why you do things. Do you want to help people find solutions, or are you mainly chasing bigger profits? Asking yourself, "Would I still do this if the money was less?" can reveal hidden motives. If the answer is "no," perhaps it is time to adjust your approach. It is not wrong to aim for profit, but faith nudges you to keep compassion at the center.

Praying over small decisions may seem odd at first—like which ad design to use—but it is not about hearing a magical voice saying "Choose the blue one." It is about inviting spiritual wisdom into your everyday tasks. You stay open to the nudge that says, "Focus on the message of hope rather than fear," or "Highlight the customer's story, not your own glory." Over time, these nudges shape an outreach style that resonates with peace and authenticity.

Gratitude for Results

Even if your marketing brings thousands of new customers, keep your heart thankful. Recognize that success is a gift. It may come from your effort, but also from the grace of circumstances, timing, and divine favor. Celebrating wins with gratitude helps prevent arrogance. You remember that you are a caretaker of your talents, using them to serve. This mindset keeps your marketing grounded in humility. And if you fail, that same attitude lets you learn and press on without losing hope.

Handling Negative Feedback with Grace

Responding to Criticism

In marketing, not everyone will love what you do. Some may leave harsh reviews, whether fairly or unfairly. Faith-based marketing means handling criticism with kindness and fairness. You do not lash out or shame the critic. Instead, you politely thank them for sharing their view and try to see if there is any truth that can help you improve. If they are upset, you can apologize for their bad experience and offer a solution, if possible.

Sometimes, people's complaints are more about their own frustrations than your work. Still, keeping a calm and gentle spirit reflects well on your brand. A wise approach is to handle problems privately—invite them to message or call you directly. People watching from the sidelines often admire a business that stays polite and caring, even when wrongly attacked.

Learning from Mistakes

There will be times when negative feedback is accurate. Perhaps your shipping was delayed, or your product arrived damaged. Admitting fault quickly can turn an upset customer into a loyal fan. Offer to make it right—refund, replace, or provide a discount on a future order. These gestures do not just fix a problem; they show you practice the same kindness you talk about in your marketing. Word of such fairness spreads, boosting your image as a trustworthy enterprise.

Forgiveness and Moving On

Some criticisms may be personal or hurtful, especially if people mock your faith-based stance. It can sting deeply. Faith teaches forgiveness, which can apply here too. Forgiving does not mean ignoring wrongdoing; it means not letting bitterness grow in your heart. If an individual repeatedly spreads lies, you may need to protect your reputation through calm explanations or legal advice. Yet, carrying rage inside helps no one. Let your spiritual roots remind you to stay compassionate, even when others are not.

Growing a Supportive Network

Collaborations with Like-Minded Entrepreneurs

You are not alone in mixing faith and marketing. Plenty of business owners value honesty, generosity, and spiritual guidance. Seek them out. Collaborations—like joint giveaways, shared blog posts, or co-hosted events—can multiply your reach. You also learn from each other's experiences. If you form a network of faith-driven peers, you gain a safe place to discuss challenges and share best practices.

Mentors Who Balance Faith and Business

Finding a mentor who has successfully merged faith with commerce can guide your outreach. They might share stories of how they handled promotional stunts or overcame moral dilemmas. A good mentor challenges you to stay strong in your convictions while still being savvy about modern marketing trends. If you cannot find someone local, look for online groups or books by entrepreneurs who live out their faith in their brand. Mentors remind you that you can flourish in marketing without abandoning your moral center.

Leaning on Community Prayer and Support

If you belong to a church or spiritual gathering, let them know your goals and struggles. Ask for their prayers when launching a new campaign or entering a tough market. Sometimes, they can also give practical help—maybe a friend in your congregation is great with design or social media. By sharing your journey, you foster a two-way street: your business can support the community, and the community supports your business. This synergy can energize your outreach, providing a broader base of encouragement.

Balancing Bold Outreach and Respect for Boundaries

Putting Yourself Out There

Having faith in your marketing does not mean hiding your business under a rock. You still need to spread the word—by running ads, sending emails, or attending trade shows. Faith-based outreach can be bold, such as hosting events that feature prayer or positive music. However, be sure your boldness does not become pushy or disrespectful.

You can be excited about your product and share how your faith guides you without making others feel pressured to believe the same. Let your audience see your enthusiasm and let them decide if they resonate with your message. Keep the door open for respectful conversations rather than forcing faith topics on uninterested people.

Respecting Different Beliefs

In a diverse world, not everyone shares your faith. Some customers might love your brand because of its honesty, but not care about your spiritual side. That is okay. Serving them well is part of living out your values—loving neighbors, near and far. If a customer asks about your faith, you can answer politely. If they do not, there is no need to push the subject. Providing excellent service can speak volumes about your character, sometimes more than words alone.

Drawing a Line Between Faith and Marketing

Though your faith shapes your heart, your marketing materials do not have to preach sermons. Many faith-based entrepreneurs mention their beliefs briefly—like a sentence about their inspiration or a small quote on the website. They keep the main focus on how they can help the customer. This balance allows you to be genuine about your faith without overshadowing the product or turning your outreach into a sermon. People who are interested may ask for more details.

Real-Life Examples of Faith in Marketing and Outreach

The Bakery That Offered Daily Encouragement

A small bakery in a quiet town decided to include a short, uplifting note with every purchase. Sometimes it was a gentle phrase like, "You are loved," or a simple verse like, "Be kind to one another." Customers started coming back not just for the fresh bread, but for the positivity. Local media noticed and featured the bakery's cheerful mission. Sales increased, but more importantly, the owner felt she was sprinkling a bit of hope into each day. Her faith motivated her to spread encouragement in a gentle way.

The Tech Startup with a Service Mindset

A tech startup founder built software to help nonprofits track donors. Instead of focusing on profit alone, she priced her product affordably for small charities. She also donated a portion of her revenue to support community groups. Her ads focused on how her software saved nonprofits time so they could serve more people, not on how cool the features were. When asked, she shared that her faith led her to empower organizations doing good work. Word spread quickly among churches and charities, and her product became a go-to solution, all without aggressive marketing.

The Fitness Coach Who Shared Spiritual Growth

A personal trainer used social media to post daily workout tips. She also included short reflections on perseverance, caring for one's body, and finding strength in faith. She never pushed religion, but she spoke naturally about how prayer helped her stay disciplined. Her page drew followers who appreciated the mix of fitness advice and gentle spiritual insights. Many joined her online coaching program to improve both body and soul. Although she was not a pastor, her faith in marketing showed through how she genuinely supported people's holistic well-being.

Spreading Light through Faithful Outreach

Faith in marketing and outreach does not mean you ignore business realities. You still plan campaigns, track metrics, and refine your messages. The difference is the heart behind it all. You see customers as real people, not just dollars. You view ads and social media posts as ways to serve, inspire, or educate, rather than simply push products. You find that each marketing step can honor God by honoring the dignity of those you hope to reach.

When you allow your faith to shape your marketing, you invite customers into a relationship built on trust. Your genuine care becomes the shining difference that draws people to your brand. You do not have to pretend or manipulate—your authenticity speaks louder than any flashy ad. Over time, your consistent kindness, honesty, and outreach efforts create a loyal community who values what you do.

Remember, faith in marketing is a journey. Some days, you might second-guess yourself, wondering if you should be more aggressive or follow the crowd. In those moments, prayer and reflection can bring you back to your core mission. You remember that your business aims to serve a higher purpose, not just fill a bank account. By taking the time to tell your story, serve your community, and keep your conscience clear, you build not only a thriving enterprise but also a legacy of love and light in the marketplace.

So, keep your marketing bright, keep your message honest, and let your faith guide your steps. Each post, flyer, or conversation can plant seeds of hope in someone's day. Each fair deal or helpful hand can restore a bit of faith in honest business practices. In doing so, you transform marketing from a pushy task into a gracious invitation— one where your business and your beliefs walk hand in hand, shining a beam of goodness for all to see.

PART V

FAITH AS A SUSTAINING FORCE

12

CELEBRATING SMALL WINS

"For who has despised the day of small things?"

(ZECHARIAH 4:10)

Finding Joy in Every Step

Imagine you are climbing a tall mountain. You look up and see the snowy peak far away. It might take days or weeks to get there, and the path can seem endless. Sometimes, you feel tired or wonder if you will ever reach the top. But what if, instead of waiting until you finish the climb, you take a moment each day to notice how far you have come? Maybe you conquered a steep trail today or spotted a beautiful sunrise you never expected. These small, happy moments can renew your energy and remind you why you started climbing in the first place.

In business and in life, it is often the same. You have big goals—maybe launching a new product, growing your team, or serving more customers. Reaching these goals can feel a little like climbing a huge mountain, with steps so small you sometimes do not see your progress. Celebrating small wins helps you notice these little victories along the way. You pause to say, "Look how far I have come!" or "I am thankful for what happened today!"

In this chapter, we will explore why celebrating small wins matters and how to do it in a way that honors your faith and values. You will discover practical methods for recognizing daily blessings, cheering on your team, and keeping your heart grateful. You will also learn how these mini-celebrations can build momentum, boost morale, and open your eyes to new possibilities. By the end, you will see that you do not have to wait for the mountain's peak to find joy; you can find it in every step you take.

What Are Small Wins?

Defining a "Win"

A small win can be any positive achievement, no matter how tiny. It might be sending an important email you have been putting off, finishing a challenging part of a project, or receiving one kind note from a customer. Sometimes, it is just getting through a tough day without giving up. A win does not have to be flashy or perfect. It is simply a sign you are moving forward.

Examples in Everyday Life

Business: You wake up, check your inbox, and see that one new customer left a glowing review. This is a win. Maybe you only sold one product today, but that one product went to a delighted buyer.

Personal: You wanted to exercise more, and you managed a ten-minute walk. That is a win, too. You might not have run a marathon, but you did more than before.

Teamwork: Your team has been struggling with communication. Today, one coworker took the initiative to clarify tasks with another. That small act might save hours of confusion tomorrow—a win worth noticing.

Why We Often Overlook Small Wins

Sometimes, we focus so much on the end goal that we forget to see the progress happening right under our noses. Our culture often praises big achievements, like hitting a major sales milestone or earning a big award. But life mostly consists of many small moments. If you only celebrate the giant victories, you might miss the little stepping stones that lead you there. By training yourself to spot these small wins, you keep your spirit uplifted and your motivation alive.

Why Celebrate Small Wins?

Motivation and Momentum

Think about pushing a heavy boulder. Getting it rolling is tough, but once it starts moving, it becomes easier to keep it going. Celebrating small wins works like that push. Each little recognition builds momentum. If you see progress daily or weekly, you stay excited and believe you can reach your bigger dreams.

Building Confidence

Small wins remind you that you are capable, even if you sometimes doubt yourself. When you see evidence of progress—like a design finished, a new client gained, or a difficult conversation handled gracefully—you realize you have what it takes. This confidence can be a shield against fear or discouragement. Over time, your self-belief grows stronger, making you more willing to tackle bigger challenges.

Encouraging Gratitude

Faith teaches us to be thankful for our blessings. Yet, in busy schedules, we might forget to pause and appreciate them. By celebrating small wins, you practice daily gratitude. You train your mind to spot the good rather than dwell on the negative. This shift in focus can lighten your heart, reduce stress, and remind you that each day holds gifts to be thankful for, even in hard times.

Fostering a Positive Team Culture

If you lead a team, celebrating small wins together boosts morale. People feel seen and appreciated. They realize their efforts matter, not just the final outcome. This atmosphere encourages them to share ideas, support each other, and approach problems with confidence. It also reduces burnout since they get little bursts of positive energy instead of waiting for one massive reward at the end.

Tying Celebration to Faith and Values

Recognizing God's Hand in Daily Life

Many faith traditions say that every good thing ultimately comes from a divine source. When you celebrate a small win, you also acknowledge the presence of God's grace in your journey. You might whisper a quick prayer of thanks or pause to reflect on how unexpected blessings came at just the right time. This habit keeps you humble and connected to a bigger story, reminding you that you are not alone in your efforts.

Serving Others Through Your Celebrations

Celebrating a small win does not always mean throwing a party for yourself. It can also be a chance to serve. Maybe your small win was finishing a project early, so you have free time to help a team member who is behind. Or your business made a modest profit this month—maybe you share a portion of that to help someone in need. By letting your faith shape how you celebrate, you turn personal victory into shared blessing.

Reflecting on Moral Lessons

Each small win might teach a lesson about patience, perseverance, kindness, or creativity. Taking a moment to reflect on these lessons can deepen your spiritual growth. For example, if you overcame a minor conflict at work by listening rather than arguing, you might later see how that experience aligns with biblical teachings about being slow to anger. Thus, a small win can also be a spiritual stepping stone, shaping your character for bigger challenges ahead.

Practical Ways to Celebrate Small Wins

Keeping a "Win Journal"

One simple tool is a "win journal." It can be a notebook, an online document, or a special app. Each day, list at least one positive outcome. Maybe you overcame a moment of fear, found a neat solution to a problem, or finished a task early. These entries do not need to be long—just a sentence or two. Over weeks and months, your journal becomes a record of grace and growth.

Idea: You could pair your win journal with a gratitude list, writing down something you are thankful for each day. This approach keeps your heart centered on both progress and blessings.

Sharing Good News with Others

Human beings are social creatures. Sometimes, telling someone about your small win amplifies the joy. It can be a friend, a coworker, or a family member. You might say, "Hey, I finally figured out that tricky software bug today!" or "We just got our first international customer!" By speaking it out loud, you give the moment more weight, and you might even receive encouraging words in return.

Caution: Make sure you keep a humble tone. There is a difference between happily sharing progress and bragging. A gentle approach is to present your win as gratitude or excitement, not "Look how great I am."

Visual Aids or Progress Boards

If you or your team love visuals, create a progress board where you mark each completed step or milestone. You could use sticky notes, color-coded magnets, or digital trackers on a big screen. Seeing these achievements pile up is motivating. It also makes it easier to show outsiders—like investors or mentors—that your project is constantly moving forward.

Team Tip: Place the board in a shared space. Each time someone moves a sticky note from "In Progress" to "Done," everyone can give a quick cheer or applause. This tiny moment can brighten the whole day.

Quick Rewards

In moderation, little rewards can be fun. Maybe you promise yourself a favorite snack, a short walk outside, or a quiet reading break each time you finish a certain task. With a team, you might bring donuts on Friday if you hit a weekly goal. These treats should not overshadow the deeper meaning of your work, but they can add an element of playful celebration to the routine.

Balanced Approach: Use rewards wisely. If everything becomes about getting a treat, people might focus more on the prize than on genuine progress. Make sure the true reward is the joy of moving forward, with a small perk on the side.

Celebrating with a Team

Team Huddles and Shout-Outs

One effective method is hosting brief, regular team huddles. In these quick meetings—maybe 10 or 15 minutes—everyone shares one thing that went well since the last meeting. It might be a personal success ("I finally organized my inbox!") or a group success ("We got a nice email from a client praising our service!"). Hearing these stories reminds everyone that progress happens in many shapes and sizes.

Encourage Inclusiveness: Make sure every voice is heard. Even quiet team members should have the chance to speak. This fosters unity and respect for all contributions, big or small.

Encouraging Peer Recognition

Celebrations mean more when they come from peers, not just from the boss. You might create a system where employees can nominate each other for small acts of kindness or problem-solving. For instance, if someone helped fix a glitch in the network, another employee can submit that as a "win" on their behalf. Once a week, you read these shout-outs aloud. This practice builds a culture of looking for and honoring each other's strengths.

Spiritual Touch in Team Celebrations

If your team is comfortable with faith references, you can include a short prayer or moment of reflection at the end of a meeting to thank God for the wins. If not everyone shares the same faith, you can still keep the atmosphere respectful. You might say something like, "I am really grateful for the progress we saw this week, and I hope we keep supporting each other." The point is to ground your celebrations in gratitude and unity, reflecting the kindness and humility that come from faith-driven leadership.

How Small Wins Fuel Larger Goals

Building Up to Bigger Milestones

Think of your big goal as a puzzle with many pieces. Each small win is like placing one puzzle piece correctly. Alone, that piece might not look like much, but as more pieces click into place, the full picture emerges. If you never celebrate placing the pieces, you might lose patience or feel lost. By noticing each piece you add, you keep the vision alive and your confidence strong.

Maintaining Morale During Long Projects

Big projects—like writing a book, opening a new branch, or completing a complex software—can span months or years. Without short-term boosts, teams might lose focus. Celebrating small wins gives fresh energy. People see tangible evidence that they are moving forward. It also helps them handle setbacks more calmly because they remember past successes and trust that new wins will come.

Avoiding the "All or Nothing" Trap

Sometimes, we get stuck thinking we have either succeeded or failed, with nothing in between. This leads to discouragement when results do not show up immediately. Celebrating small wins shifts your mindset to see life as a journey filled with steps, not a single finish line. If you lose one client, it does not mean total failure. You still have the small achievements of retaining other clients or improving your service. Step by step, you gather enough small victories to shape a bigger success story.

Overcoming Obstacles to Celebration

Perfectionism

One major obstacle is perfectionism, the belief that only "flawless" success counts as worth celebrating. If you always demand perfection, you might ignore small gains because they do not measure up to your high bar. But faith reminds us that we grow in stages. Nobody is perfect on day one. By embracing the beauty of small, imperfect steps, you free yourself to enjoy the journey.

> *Tip: If you sense perfectionism creeping in, try setting a daily or weekly "wins goal." Challenge yourself to find at least one thing, no matter how small, that went right. Over time, you retrain your mind to see progress as valuable.*

Lack of Time or Awareness

Another obstacle is simply forgetting to notice wins because you are too busy. The day ends, you are exhausted, and you have not paused to reflect. To fix this, make celebration a habit. Set an alarm at the end of the workday to spend five minutes reviewing achievements. Or add a small question to your daily planner: "What went well today?" A little prompt can spark awareness.

Fear of Pride

Some people worry that celebrating wins is bragging. They do not want to appear self-centered or boastful. Yet, healthy celebration can be done humbly. You can say, "I am grateful for this progress," rather than "I am so amazing." If you are leading a team, you can spotlight your members' efforts, praising God or good fortune for the help along the way. Remember, celebrating does not have to mean shouting "I am the best!" It can simply be giving thanks for small blessings.

Integrating Faith into Personal Celebration

Daily Devotions or Quiet Time

If faith is central to your life, consider blending celebration with daily devotions. After reading Scripture or a spiritual text, spend a minute listing blessings or achievements. You might say a quick prayer: "Thank You, Lord, for giving me the strength to make that phone call," or "I am grateful for the patience I found during a tough meeting today." This practice ties your work life to your spiritual life, keeping them aligned.

Worship and Acknowledgment

In some traditions, worship services may set aside moments for testimonies—short stories of God's goodness. Sharing a small work-related win, like "We overcame a supply issue this week," can encourage others who face similar struggles. This public testimony also humbles you, as you attribute success to God's guidance, not just your own cleverness.

Journaling with Prayer

We mentioned a "win journal" earlier. Another step is adding a prayer component. After noting each win, write a brief prayer of thanks or reflection. "Lord, I saw progress in my marketing plan. Please guide my next steps." This prayerful approach helps you remain connected to your purpose and values, ensuring you do not drift into pride or forget the One who provides your opportunities.

Sharing Celebrations with Customers

Being Transparent About Milestones

Customers enjoy feeling part of your story. If you hit a small milestone—like shipping your 100th order or welcoming your 20th client—consider sharing the good news on social media or email newsletters. Thank your customers for helping you reach that point. This approach shows you value their role in your success. It also spreads positivity, reminding people that your brand cherishes each step.

Inviting Customer Involvement

You can also invite customers to celebrate their own small wins. For example, if you sell fitness gear, ask them to share a photo after completing a short workout. If you provide art supplies, encourage them to post a simple drawing they finished. By shining a spotlight on your customers' achievements, you build a community of mutual support. People see your brand as a place of encouragement, not just transactions.

Humility and Respect in Public Celebrations

When sharing wins publicly, maintain humility. Let your tone reflect thankfulness, acknowledging your team, customers, and faith. Avoid sounding arrogant or patting yourself on the back too much. People appreciate sincerity. If your message is: "We are deeply thankful for each step forward, and we hope to serve you even better," it resonates more than "Look how awesome we are!" Emphasize that these small wins motivate you to keep growing and helping others.

Real-Life Stories of Small Wins Leading to Big Change

The Coffee Shop That Kept a Gratitude Board

In a small-town coffee shop, the owner put a large chalkboard on the wall, labeling it "Today's Wins." Each day, she wrote something positive—like "Tried a new latte recipe!" or "Received a sweet thank-you note from a customer." Customers also wrote their own little wins, such as "Finished my homework!" or "Met a new friend!" Over time, the board became a mini community of gratitude. People looked forward to seeing new notes and adding their own. This sense of shared celebration helped the coffee shop stand out and become a beloved spot in the neighborhood.

A Tech Start-Up's Weekly "High-Five Fridays"

A tech start-up faced intense pressure to develop software quickly. Team members often felt drained. The founder decided every Friday afternoon, they would pause for "High-Five Fridays." Each employee named one small accomplishment from the week. Some said, "I finally fixed that bug," or "I learned a new coding trick." Others said, "I overcame my fear of presenting in the team meeting." Everyone gave a virtual or literal high five. This small ritual boosted morale, and the software project moved forward steadily because people felt recognized. Eventually, the start-up launched successfully, crediting their culture of celebrating daily progress.

A Personal Journey in Overcoming Fear

A freelance writer struggled with anxiety over sending pitches to big magazines. She often froze, worried about rejection. A mentor advised her to celebrate each pitch emailed, regardless of the outcome. So, she created a small reward system: for every pitch she sent, she marked it on a calendar and allowed herself ten minutes of her favorite music playlist. Over time, the calendar filled with marks, and her fear lessened. She sold more articles than ever, but the real victory was learning to celebrate the act of trying, not just the acceptance letters.

Troubleshooting Common Problems

"I Celebrate, but I Still Feel Stuck"

Sometimes, you recognize small wins but still feel trapped. Perhaps your progress is slower than you hoped. In this case, reflect on whether your goals are realistic or if you need more support or training. Celebrating small wins is not a magic fix; it is part of a healthy mindset. Combine it with seeking advice from mentors or revising your plan if you are truly stuck. Yet, keep celebrating any forward motion—it might be less than you want, but it is still progress.

"My Team Thinks Celebrations Are Silly"

Not everyone is used to pausing for small victories. They might see it as childish or a waste of time. Try explaining why it matters: it keeps morale high, helps us see growth, and aligns with our faith-based values of gratitude. Start with simple, low-key methods, like adding a short "win" section at the end of a meeting. Over time, as they experience the uplift, they may warm up to the idea.

"We Celebrate, but Then We Slip Back to Old Habits"

Maintaining a culture of celebration can be challenging. Maybe you started strong, but after a busy season, everyone fell back into focusing only on big goals. Revisit your routines. Perhaps you need a consistent structure, like a "Win Wednesday" reminder or a monthly reflection day. Keep the practice alive by mixing in new approaches—invite different team members to lead the celebration or use fun themes. Consistency in small celebrations eventually becomes second nature.

A Life Enriched by Small Victories

Celebrating small wins is more than just a motivational trick. It is a way of life, rooted in faith and gratitude. It reminds you that progress happens one step at a time, and each step matters. It keeps your mind attentive to the quiet blessings that often get drowned out by worries or big ambitions. It also shapes your business culture, turning it into a place where hope thrives and each person's contribution is valued.

As you continue your journey—whether building a business, improving a skill, or growing in character—make it a habit to pause and say, "That was a win." Let your faith guide you to appreciate how God's hand works in small ways, opening doors or sending help right when it is needed. Celebrate with others, encouraging them to notice their own steps forward. Over time, these mini-celebrations weave together into a tapestry of joy and thankfulness, fueling you to climb even higher mountains with confidence.

When the big achievements eventually come—a product launch, a best-selling book, or a thriving community—you will see they are made up of countless small wins along the way. And if you have been celebrating all along, you will reach the peak with a grateful heart, well-practiced in finding goodness in every stage. That is the beauty of celebrating small wins. You do not wait for the end; you savor the journey, knowing each step is a blessing worth cherishing.

13

LEARNING FROM FAILURE

"Though he fall, he shall not be utterly cast down; for the LORD upholds him with His hand."

(PSALM 37:24)

The Unexpected Teacher

Have you ever tried something new—a project, a hobby, or even a small business idea—only to watch it collapse before it could take off? Maybe your carefully planned product did not sell, or a big client canceled at the last minute. In those moments, you might feel embarrassment, frustration, or even shame. It can feel like the end of the road. Yet, in many faith traditions, there is a surprising message: failure is not final. In fact, it can be one of your greatest teachers.

Think about babies learning to walk. They stumble, fall, and get up again. Each tumble helps them figure out how to balance better the next time. Soon enough, those wobbly steps turn into confident strides. The same principle applies when you "fail" in business or any area of life. If you allow it, each failure can help you grow stronger, wiser, and more creative. You discover what does not work and adapt. You learn humility and empathy for others who struggle. Over time, these lessons can guide you toward bigger successes than you ever imagined.

In this chapter, we will explore how failure can actually become a stepping stone. You will see how faith can shape your view of setbacks, turning them from dead ends into open doors of opportunity. We will look at practical ways to analyze what went wrong, build resilience, and stay hopeful in the face of disappointment. By the end, you will realize that failure does not have to be the final word; it can be the spark that leads you to a fresh start. Let us begin by digging deeper into what failure really is—and what it is not.

Redefining Failure

Failure vs. Learning Experience

Many people think of failure as "the end." You tried and did not reach your goal, so that is it. But what if we saw it differently? What if we viewed a failure as a learning experience that points us in a new direction? This shift in thinking is powerful. It reminds you that messing up is not a permanent label on your identity; it is just a moment of not-yet.

Imagine you open a lemonade stand on a rainy day, and barely anyone shows up. You could feel bad and say, "I am a horrible entrepreneur." Or you could say, "I learned that location and weather matter. Next time, I will choose a sunny weekend at a busier spot." One approach leads to quitting; the other leads to growth.

Faith's Perspective on Mistakes

In many faith traditions, mistakes and failures are seen as part of our human journey. They are not proof you are worthless, but signs you are imperfect and still growing. The Bible, for instance, is full of stories of people who failed big time—like Moses who lost his temper, or Peter who denied knowing Jesus. Yet, God still worked through them, transforming their failures into testimony. This suggests that failure might be exactly where divine grace meets your effort, shaping your character and steering you back on track.

Failure as a Normal Part of Growth

Consider sports. Even the best basketball players miss shots, the best baseball hitters strike out, and the best gymnasts fall off the beam.

Failure is baked into the process of getting better. In business, you might lose money on a marketing campaign or launch a product that flops. Accepting this as normal frees you to try again without shame. Each attempt refines your skills. Over time, those so-called "failures" become stepping stones to mastery.

Common Fears Around Failure

Fear of Judgment

Sometimes, the real sting of failure is worrying about what others think. You might dread the eye-rolls, the whispered comments like, "I knew they would not make it." But remember, many successful people faced loads of skepticism before their breakthrough. If you let fear of judgment control you, you might never explore new ideas. Your faith can remind you that you answer to a higher calling than just public opinion. God's perspective—full of mercy and second chances—matters more than gossip.

Fear of Lost Resources

When a business idea fails, you can lose money, time, or even relationships. These losses hurt. Yet, consider them as investments in your education. You paid tuition in the "school of failure," learning lessons you could not learn otherwise. For instance, you might find a better way to budget, discover new marketing approaches, or realize you need a mentor's guidance. By reframing these losses as tuition rather than destruction, you allow yourself to move on with less regret.

Fear of Letting Down Others

You might worry about disappointing your family, friends, or coworkers who believed in you. That pressure can feel heavy. But true supporters rarely abandon you just because you stumbled. They understand that life is full of twists. Communicating openly about your lessons and your next steps can reassure them. Show how you plan to use this failure to grow smarter, stronger, and more determined. Often, that honesty deepens their respect for you rather than diminishes it.

Embracing a Faith-Filled Approach to Failure

Trusting a Bigger Plan

Faith teaches that our lives are part of a larger story. Even when plans fail, a bigger hand may be guiding us to a different path. Perhaps you tried to get a certain client or job, and it fell through. Later, you find a better opportunity you never imagined. Keeping your heart open to the possibility that God might be rerouting you can ease the pain of disappointment. Instead of "I am doomed," you can say, "Maybe this door closed, but another door might open."

Asking for Wisdom

Before, during, and after a failure, prayer or meditation can bring clarity. You might say, "God, please show me what I need to learn here," or "Give me strength to keep going." By acknowledging your need for divine guidance, you step away from pride. You also tap into a source of comfort that helps you remain calm during storms. This calmness often leads to better problem-solving and creative thinking.

Recognizing Grace in Mistakes

Grace is the idea that you can find forgiveness and fresh starts—even if you messed up badly. This is a core belief in many faiths. Maybe you made an ethical slip, lost your temper, or neglected your team, and now the business is suffering. Owning the mistake is crucial, but so is remembering that you are not beyond redemption. With humility, you can apologize, seek help, and begin anew. You do not have to stay stuck in shame or regret forever.

Turning Mistakes into Lessons

Analyze What Went Wrong

After a failure, one of the best steps you can take is to do a calm, detailed review of what happened. Ask questions like:

- Did I research the market enough?
- Were my costs too high?
- Did I communicate poorly with partners or customers?
- Did a personal issue (like stress or distraction) affect my decisions?

Be honest but not cruel to yourself. The goal is to uncover the real reasons behind the flop, not to beat yourself up. By seeing the true causes, you can fix them next time.

Identify What Went Right

Believe it or not, failures often contain some bright spots. Maybe your design was praised even if the pricing was off. Or your marketing message resonated with a small group, suggesting you have a niche audience. Finding these small sparks of success helps you salvage the good parts of your plan. You do not throw out everything—just the pieces that did not work.

Create a Learning Document

Consider writing a "Lessons Learned" summary. It can be a page or two listing the main takeaways: what you would do differently, what to avoid, and what to keep. Refer to this document the next time you launch a similar project. Better yet, share it with your team if you have one. This transforms failure into a guidebook for the future, raising your chances of success next time.

Building Resilience and Persistence

The Power of Resilience

Resilience is the ability to bounce back after you fall. It is not about never falling—it is about standing up each time, a bit wiser than before. People with strong resilience do not see failure as a reflection of their worth. They view it as a challenge to be overcome. Faith can anchor your resilience by telling you that your identity goes beyond your achievements. You are still valued and loved, no matter how many projects fail.

Small Steps Forward

If your failure shook your confidence, start rebuilding with small, manageable steps. Maybe you create a mini version of your previous project, test it with a few customers, and gather feedback. Each small success can restore your belief in your abilities. This approach also helps you refine your idea before committing big resources again. Step by step, you regain momentum and courage.

Surrounding Yourself with Support

Resilience is easier when you have people cheering you on. Friends, mentors, or a faith community can offer prayers, advice, or a listening ear. Do not isolate yourself out of shame; let others help. Talking through your feelings can lighten the load, and you might discover fresh perspectives. Sometimes, the right mentor or partner can turn your failure into a success story by giving you the insight you lacked.

Overcoming the Shame of Failure

Separating Failure from Identity

It is easy to say, "I failed, so I am a failure." But that is not true. Failing at a business venture is an event, not a label on who you are as a person. Remember your positive qualities—the strengths you bring to the table. Your faith can remind you that you are more than your mistakes. If God sees value in you, you can, too. Let that sense of worth shield you from the shame that tries to stick to you after a setback.

Confessing and Forgiving

If your failure involved moral or ethical lapses, shame may feel particularly strong. You might need to make amends, apologize to those affected, or seek forgiveness from God or others. This process is hard, but it cleans the wound, allowing you to heal. Holding onto guilt can paralyze you. Confession and forgiveness, whether spiritual or interpersonal, can free you to learn from your error and move forward with a clear conscience.

Allowing Others to Share Their Failures

Be open about your own struggles, and encourage others to do the same. This shared honesty fosters a culture where mistakes are not hidden but used for growth. If you lead a team, show vulnerability by admitting when you have messed up. This invites them to be honest about their failures, too, leading to problem-solving rather than blame. Shame loses its grip when everyone sees failure as part of the learning process rather than a taboo.

Real-Life Stories of Redemption

The Famous Failure Turned Success

Many of today's big names in business have stories of early failures. Consider Walt Disney, who was fired from a newspaper job because they said he "lacked imagination." Or Colonel Sanders, whose fried chicken recipe was rejected hundreds of times before a restaurant accepted it. These stories remind us that behind major triumphs often lie multiple failures. The difference is they did not quit. They learned, adapted, and kept knocking on doors.

Small Business Owner Who Rose Again

A friend once started a café with high hopes but had to close within a year due to low foot traffic. She lost money and felt devastated.

However, she spent the next few months analyzing local coffee trends and realized there was a big demand for specialty teas. She opened a smaller shop focused on tea blends. Her unique angle attracted loyal customers, and the business thrived. Looking back, she says the first café's closure taught her exactly how to adjust her second attempt.

Personal Moral Failure Leading to Growth

A manager lost his temper publicly at a company event, embarrassing his team and tarnishing the brand's image. He was called in by upper management and given a stern warning. Instead of quitting or denying, he apologized, sought counseling to handle stress, and asked a mentor for guidance. Over the next year, he rebuilt trust with his team, openly discussing better communication methods. His transformation was so clear that the company eventually promoted him, noting how he turned a failure into a profound learning experience.

Practical Steps After a Failure

Pause and Reflect

Before racing into a new plan, take a moment of calm. Pray or reflect. Let the dust settle and your emotions cool. Journaling can help you get thoughts on paper. Ask God or your inner wisdom for direction. This pause prevents you from making knee-jerk moves fueled by fear or anger.

Gather Feedback

Talk to customers, team members, or anyone involved in the failed endeavor. Ask them what worked and what did not. You might discover a small tweak could have saved the project. Or maybe the feedback confirms you need a totally new direction. Either way, hearing multiple viewpoints broadens your perspective.

Draft a Recovery or Next-Step Plan

Take the lessons and create a short plan:

- What will I do differently next time?
- Which resources do I need?
- Who can help or advise me?
- What timeline makes sense?

Keep it realistic and flexible. Then act on it step by step. Even if you decide to pivot to a new venture entirely, use the insights from your failure to guide you. Each bullet point in your plan should connect to a lesson you just learned.

Celebrate Progress

It might sound odd to celebrate after failing, but each time you fix a mistake, you move closer to success. Notice any small victories in your recovery process: "I found a cheaper supplier," "I pitched my idea more clearly this time," or "I handled a tough conversation with grace." These mini achievements build hope and remind you that you are not stuck in failure forever.

Learning to Trust Again

Rebuilding Self-Confidence

A big failure can shake your self-confidence. You might doubt your instincts or fear making decisions. Faith can help you trust that your mind is still capable of good ideas. Yes, you erred, but do not ignore the good you done in the past. Recall times you succeeded, even in small tasks. Bit by bit, reclaim your confidence by taking small risks again.

Trusting Others

If your failure involved a broken partnership, you might feel wary of trusting people again. While caution is wise, isolating yourself is not. Learn from the betrayal, if that is what happened, but stay open to forming new alliances. Faith teaches forgiveness, not blind naivety.

Vet new partners carefully, but do not shut out the possibility that others can uplift you.

Trusting God's Plan

Finally, a key lesson is trusting God even when you cannot see the path ahead. If your dream collapsed, it might not mean your entire calling is invalid. Perhaps you need a different approach, a different audience, or more preparation. Trust that failures can refine you. As the proverb says, "A righteous person falls seven times and rises again." Lean on prayer, scripture, or fellowship to keep your spirit steady as you wait for the next open door.

Encouraging a Failure-Friendly Culture

Leading by Example

If you run a team, your attitude toward failure sets the tone. Share your own flops and what you learned. When a team member fails, help them analyze the issue rather than just handing out punishment. This does not mean ignoring consequences, but focusing on learning more than blame. Over time, your group becomes braver about experimenting, knowing that mistakes can be stepping stones, not sinkholes.

Healthy Risk-Taking

A culture that sees failure as learning fosters healthy risk-taking. People dare to try new ideas or suggest improvements without fear of being mocked. This atmosphere can lead to breakthroughs. Of course, set boundaries—do not encourage reckless choices that ignore logic. But do give your team room to experiment, and if something goes wrong, treat it as a lesson.

Creating a Fail-Forward Mindset

"Fail-forward" means taking what you learned and applying it to the next round quickly. Instead of lingering in regret, you say, "Okay, that did not work, so let us adapt." Document insights, share them with colleagues, and roll them into the next project. This approach speeds up growth. It also honors a faith-based view that mistakes do not define your future—they inform it.

Reflection and Prayer After a Failure

Finding Quiet

After a significant failure, chaos can fill your mind. Setting aside a quiet time for reflection or prayer is soothing. You might find a peaceful spot, light a candle if that helps you focus, and speak honestly about your feelings—disappointment, anger, confusion—to God. This vulnerable conversation can bring solace and sometimes spark new ideas or comfort.

Reaffirming Your Purpose

Ask yourself, "What is my deeper calling?" Perhaps you started a business to help people, support a family, or fulfill a passion. That purpose does not vanish just because one attempt failed. Revisit your core motivation and let it ground you. If your purpose is still valid, then keep going. If you sense it is time to shift, do so, but keep an eye on how your gifts can still bless others.

Embracing Hope

Faith centers on hope—the belief that good can emerge from darkness. Even if your business or project lies in ruins, there can be seeds of future success hidden inside. Sometimes, the best ideas come when all else fails and you are forced to think differently. Praying for hope invites a mindset that sees beyond present troubles to the possibilities of tomorrow.

Falling Forward, Rising Higher

Failure can seem like a bitter end, but from a faith-driven viewpoint, it can be the birthplace of new beginnings. Every stumble offers a chance to learn, grow, and refine your approach. Embracing failure as a teacher keeps you humble and resilient. You understand that life's journey is full of ups and downs—yet, none of those downs have to define you permanently.

In business, small flops might lead to major pivots that unlock success. Personal missteps can prompt you to build healthier habits or relationships. Even moral failings can become milestones of repentance and transformation, showing how divine grace can turn shame into testimony. By learning from failure, you channel your energy not into regret, but into redemption.

As you move forward, remember:

- **Redefine Failure:** It is an event, not your identity.
- **Overcome Fear:** Do not let judgment or loss stop you from trying again.
- **Apply Faith:** Trust that a bigger story is at work, even when a door closes.
- **Extract Lessons:** Analyze what went wrong and what went right.
- **Persevere:** Resilience and support help you rise stronger and wiser.

No matter how badly you have fallen, your next step can lead you upward if you choose to learn, adapt, and trust. Failure is not a brick wall—it is a hurdle on the track, one you can leap over with grace and determination. Keep your faith alive, stay humble, and press on. In the end, the journey shaped by lessons from failure might bring you to a place far better than you ever dreamed.

14

THE LONGEVITY OF A FAITH-BASED BUSINESS

*"Unless the LORD builds the house,
the builders labor in vain."*

(PSALM 127:1)

A Firm Foundation for the Future

You stand on the threshold of tomorrow, eager to build a business that not only thrives today but continues to flourish for years to come. Yet, the business world can be turbulent. Markets shift, customer tastes change, and sudden events—from economic downturns to global crises—can knock down even strong companies. How can you ensure that your venture does not just survive the storms but remains steady for decades, maybe even generations?

A faith-based business carries an extra layer of purpose. It is not just about profits or market share. It is about living out values rooted in something greater than yourself—principles like honesty, compassion, and service. These beliefs do more than guide daily decisions. They also help your company endure when challenges arise. By leaning on these spiritual foundations, you create a business model that holds strong against the winds of change. Indeed, your faith can breathe life into your work, sustaining it in good times and bad.

In this chapter, we will explore how faith influences the long-term success of a business. We will look at practical steps you can take to remain relevant, keep learning, and expand your impact while staying rooted in spiritual principles. You will see how leaving a legacy does not happen by accident—it is the fruit of careful planning, consistent values, and a readiness to adapt. By the end, you will have a roadmap for ensuring that your faith-based business stands firm through the decades, shining as a beacon of purpose and service for future generations.

The Roots That Go Deep

Why Values Become Anchors

Think of your business as a tree. The trunk, branches, and leaves represent your products, services, and day-to-day operations. The roots, deep underground, stand for your core values—such as integrity, kindness, and faith in a guiding power. When storms come, it is not fancy leaves that keep a tree upright, but strong, deep roots. In the same way, your business can survive sudden market shifts or tough competition if it stands firmly on unwavering values.

When ethics and faith shape your choices, you avoid chasing every flashy trend that lacks substance. Instead, you weigh each opportunity against what you believe is right. This steady moral compass builds trust with customers and employees. Over time, such trust is priceless, acting like an anchor that holds you steady while rivals who sacrifice values for quick gains may drift or sink.

Faith as a Steadying Force

The business world can feel like a roller coaster—one quarter you might see strong sales, the next you might face a sudden downturn. A faith-based mindset helps you stay calm and hopeful. You remember that money, while necessary, is not the ultimate measure of success. Even if profits dip, you do not lose heart because your deeper aim is serving God and loving people. This viewpoint preserves your peace and helps you make wise decisions instead of panicking.

People sense your stability. Customers may remain loyal because they see you are not ruled by fear or greed. Employees appreciate working for someone who keeps a cool head in crisis. That stability can translate into lasting success, as your calm presence fosters loyalty, collaboration, and creative thinking—key ingredients for any business with big dreams.

Building a Legacy Over Time

A faith-based business does not just strive for next year's profit. It aims for long-term impact—sometimes even beyond the founder's lifetime. When your guiding vision extends further than your own career, you make decisions that can outlast you. For instance, you might invest in ethical supply chains, trusting that God rewards honest dealings even if it costs more short-term. You might focus on developing younger leaders in your company, ensuring that when you retire, others carry on the mission.

This legacy mindset keeps you from chasing only short-term rewards. It also reminds you that your work can be part of God's bigger plan, shaping the community and the marketplace in positive ways long after you are gone. Such a perspective can transform your business into a living testimony of faith, love, and service for future generations to see.

Continuous Learning and Adaptation

Embracing Change Without Losing Core Values

While your values remain solid, your methods can and should evolve over time. Many companies fade away because they refuse to update their strategies. A faith-based entrepreneur understands that God may open new doors or lead you down unexpected paths. You can welcome these changes without worrying about losing your essence. After all, the early apostles adapted their methods—like traveling to different lands or writing letters—while keeping the same message of hope.

In practice, this means staying alert to shifts in your industry. If customers now prefer online shopping, you explore e-commerce. If social media is the main communication channel, you learn those tools. You do not cling to old ways out of fear. Instead, you pray for wisdom to spot new trends and keep your mission relevant to modern needs.

The Value of Ongoing Education

Longevity hinges on your willingness to keep learning. Technology changes fast, consumer habits move in cycles, and global events can alter entire markets overnight. A faith-based leader does not assume they know everything or rely solely on tradition. Instead, you adopt a humble posture: "Lord, teach me how to serve effectively in this evolving world." That means attending workshops, reading books, and seeking mentorship.

Look for mentors who share your values but also have strengths in new areas—like digital marketing, customer analytics, or sustainable packaging. Encourage your team to stay curious, too. Offer training or cover some cost for online courses. As everyone grows in knowledge, your business remains creative and adaptable, ready to pivot whenever challenges come.

Integrating Faith with Innovation

Some people think faith and innovation do not mix. They assume that trusting God means doing things the "old-fashioned" way. In truth, many faith-based pioneers throughout history used their creativity to solve pressing problems—like building hospitals, inventing printing presses, or designing new farming techniques. Leaning on faith does not mean staying stuck; it means you ask God to inspire fresh ideas.

You might pray before brainstorming sessions, asking for divine sparks of wisdom. You might read Scripture or inspirational stories that remind you how God works in unexpected ways. A company committed to serving others and honoring God can be the perfect environment for bold invention. Over time, these innovations can keep your venture at the forefront of the market, ensuring a bright future even when others fade.

Nurturing Future Leaders

Passing the Torch

A key to longevity is ensuring that new leaders will eventually take your place and continue the mission. If your business depends solely on you—your energy, ideas, and personal brand—it might struggle or collapse when you retire or pursue another path. Faith teaches us about mentorship and discipleship: guiding the next generation to carry the light forward.

In your organization, you can create clear paths for team members who show promise. This could mean giving them more responsibility over a small project, providing leadership training, or involving them in strategic planning. If you see someone who aligns with your values, invest in them. Let them learn from your successes and your mistakes. Over time, they can grow into wise leaders who honor God and uphold the business's foundation long after you step back.

Teaching Core Values

It is one thing to hire skilled people; it is another to ensure they share the heart of your vision. A faith-based business thrives when employees, especially future leaders, embrace the same moral principles that guide you—like honesty, kindness, respect, and diligence. Make your values part of everyday life at work. Hold short devotions, or at least offer an open forum for discussing ethical dilemmas.

Lead by example, showing that these values are not just words but shape your decisions. Over time, a culture forms—a "way we do things here"—that new team members absorb. If the next leaders truly get these values, they will handle the business with the same care and conviction that built it, ensuring continuity and trustworthiness across generations.

Balancing Authority and Service

A faith-based approach to leadership often emphasizes serving those you lead. This style fosters deep loyalty and a genuine desire to keep the business going strong. Teach your budding leaders that being "in charge" means helping others reach their goals, not bossing them around. By cultivating servant-leaders, you make the workplace healthier and reduce turnover. People will be more willing to stay for years if they feel respected and valued. The next wave of leadership, molded by these ideals, will thus keep your legacy alive and well.

Fostering Customer and Community Loyalty

Building Trust Through Consistency

Longevity depends heavily on customer trust. When people know that you stand by your promises, treat them fairly, and hold fast to your moral standards, they return year after year. A faith-based business can excel here by consistently reflecting the character of God—reliable, caring, and honest. If a customer has an issue with your product, you do not brush them off or deny responsibility. You handle it with empathy and a desire to make it right. Over time, they see your business as more than just a store or service—it feels like a friend.

Engaging the Local Community

Even in a global age, local support matters. Faith-driven businesses often see themselves as part of a bigger neighborhood family. They sponsor local events, support charities, or volunteer in community projects. By doing so, you root your business in real relationships. When times are hard—like during an economic slump or natural disaster—your community may stand by you because you stood by them. This mutual care fosters resilience.

Moreover, these partnerships can grow your reputation and broaden your network. A local church or nonprofit might recommend your services to their members, or local leaders might appreciate your contributions and offer public support. This synergy between faith-based values and civic engagement can keep your brand strong for decades.

Evolving with Customer Needs

Serving the same community for years means you must keep pace with their changing needs. If you sold the same products in the same way forever, you might become irrelevant. Instead, you listen: ask customers what they want, observe trends, and adapt your offerings. This might involve adding new product lines, redesigning your service process, or shifting how you communicate (maybe moving to an app or online platform). Faith-driven longevity is not about staying stuck in the past—it is about carrying timeless principles into new seasons of life and commerce.

Financial Stewardship and Sustainability

Honoring God with Finances

Faith-based businesses often recognize that the resources they hold are blessings to be managed wisely. This perspective changes how you handle money. You avoid reckless spending or gambling on high-risk schemes. You also steer clear of shady financial practices because integrity matters more than a quick dollar. By keeping honest books, paying bills on time, and treating suppliers fairly, you lay down a trustworthy financial bedrock that can sustain you over the long run.

Planning for the Future

One reason many businesses fail is a lack of financial planning. A faith-based owner, trusting in God's provision, still needs to do their part in planning. This might mean setting aside emergency funds, diversifying income streams, or purchasing adequate insurance. Yes, you rely on faith, but you also use common sense. Just as Joseph in the Bible stored grain during the good years for the famine to come, you can build reserves and prepare for downturns. This responsible approach ensures you have the means to weather surprises.

Balancing Profit and Purpose

Striving for profit is not wrong, but if chasing profit becomes the sole aim, you risk drifting from your faith-based mission. Longevity arises when you strike a balance—earning enough to invest in growth, reward employees, and support your family, while still keeping moral and spiritual priorities at the forefront. This might mean turning down a lucrative deal if it compromises your ethics or setting aside funds for charitable work. Over time, such a balanced approach can deepen loyalty and respect from both employees and customers, boosting your brand's longevity.

Overcoming Challenges to Longevity

Navigating Leadership Changes

Over decades, leadership will shift. You might pass the baton to a trusted partner or a younger generation. Conflict or confusion can arise if there is no clear plan. Faith-based businesses do well to prepare a succession strategy early. Include spiritual and ethical guidelines, so new leaders know the core values they must uphold. This clarity helps avoid power struggles that can tear a company apart.

Handling External Threats

From sudden economic recessions to unexpected global events like pandemics, external threats can strain your business. Prayer and strategic planning can work hand in hand. While you trust God's sovereignty, you also create backup plans—like pivoting to online sales, reorganizing your supply chain, or temporarily scaling back costs. Your faith helps you stay hopeful; your planning helps you remain practical. Together, they form a shield against panic when the outside world changes fast.

Maintaining Spiritual Fervor

Sometimes, as businesses mature, the original zeal for serving God and others can fade. People get comfortable, or routine overshadows vision. To keep your spiritual fire alive, schedule regular times for reflection—company retreats, devotional segments in meetings, or personal prayer. Revisit the stories of how your business began, how God guided you, and the testimony of changed lives along the way. Such reminders rekindle passion, ensuring you do not become a "good company" that forgot the deeper reason for its birth.

Leaving a Legacy That Lasts

Beyond the Founder

You might dream of your business continuing long after you are gone. A true legacy is about passing on your faith-driven mission to the next generation of leaders, workers, and customers. Encourage a culture that celebrates both tradition and innovation. If the founder's name and face are everywhere, the company might struggle once you step away. But if employees and the community feel ownership of the vision, they can carry it forward with pride.

Documenting Your Principles

To ensure longevity, document the core beliefs and practices that define your business. This might be a simple "Faith and Values Handbook" or a set of guiding statements displayed on the office wall. It could list how you handle disputes, how you treat customers, or how you honor God in day-to-day tasks. This written record becomes a north star, helping future staff—who might never meet you in person—uphold the same standards and spirit you built from the start.

Investing in the Next Generation

Some faith-based entrepreneurs go beyond their own company, mentoring young adults or sponsoring educational programs. By investing in people's growth, you create a ripple effect. Maybe you host workshops where aspiring business owners learn about values-based leadership. Or you might fund scholarships for local kids who want to study ethical business management. These outreach efforts keep your mission alive in new hearts and minds, ensuring that even if your company evolves or merges, the essence of your faith-driven passion spreads far and wide.

Real-Life Testimonials of Enduring Faith-Based Ventures

Family Bakery Through Generations

A small-town bakery opened eighty years ago by a faithful couple who prayed over each recipe, believing their business would bring joy to the neighborhood. They treated every customer like family, always giving an extra roll to hungry kids. Decades later, their grandchildren run the bakery, still using the same recipes and friendly approach. Locals remain loyal because they taste not just sweetness but kindness in every loaf. Through wars, recessions, and changing diets, the bakery persevered by staying true to its founding values of love and generosity.

High-Tech Firm with a Servant Leader Mindset

In a bustling city, a faith-based tech firm emerged. The founder insisted on praying before major product launches, not out of show, but to seek wisdom and peace. He also set up a policy that a portion of every software sale went to support community programs. Twenty-five years on, the firm's pioneering software has changed many industries, but its core purpose—serving both clients and society—remains. Employees say they value the stability and ethical guidance, which helps them innovate boldly without losing compassion. This firm's name is now recognized worldwide, known for combining cutting-edge solutions with an unshakeable moral stance.

Agricultural Venture That Respects the Land

A group of farmers started a cooperative, guided by their faith that the earth is God's creation, meant to be cared for. They chose sustainable practices, rotating crops and minimizing chemicals, even when it seemed more expensive. At first, they struggled. But over time, consumers grew to respect their commitment, especially as environmental concerns rose.

The cooperative expanded, training younger farmers in eco-friendly methods. Now, the brand is a symbol of stewardship—showing that faith-driven respect for creation can yield not only healthy food but a lasting enterprise that spares the land for future generations.

Actions You Can Take Right Now

Craft or Update Your Vision Statement

Put pen to paper (or fingers to keyboard) and write a clear, concise statement of your business's faith-based goals. How do you aim to serve people, honor God, and impact the world? Keep it short enough that you can memorize it. Post it where your team can see. This statement becomes a guiding light, reminding everyone why you exist and what kind of future you are building.

Evaluate Your Adaptability

Ask yourself: "Am I willing to pivot when the market changes?" or "Do I keep learning new skills?" If the answer is "not really," decide how to become more flexible. Maybe sign up for an online course, attend a seminar, or set time aside for brainstorming. A business that refuses to adapt may survive a while, but rarely stands the test of decades.

Identify Future Leaders

Look at your current team or network. Who shows promise, a love for your values, and leadership potential? Start guiding them now. Offer mentoring sessions or let them lead a small project. By growing their confidence and abilities, you secure your business's future. They become the next torchbearers of your faith-driven mission.

Build a Succession Plan

Even if retirement feels far away, think about who will run the show when you leave. Write a basic plan: roles, responsibilities, and the spiritual values that must remain intact. This ensures that if anything happens—health issues, new life stages, or God calling you elsewhere—your business does not collapse. People will know the chain of command and the standards to uphold.

Strengthen Community Ties

Check your current involvement in the local area. Could you donate time, products, or money to a cause that resonates with your faith? Could you partner with a local group, hosting an event or providing expertise? By deepening community roots, you create a support system that can bolster your enterprise for years to come.

A Lasting Light

Building a faith-based business is like lighting a candle that can burn through the night. The flame is not just about making profits, but shining hope, integrity, and service into the marketplace. Yet, a candle can flicker if not cared for. Lasting success requires constant attention to your values, your people, and your evolving environment. You must keep trimming the wick (removing outdated methods), adding wax (investing in new ideas), and shielding the flame from strong winds (upholding your core beliefs).

The good news is that your faith offers both a foundation and a compass. It provides the moral roots to hold you steady and the guiding sense that your work is part of something bigger than money or fame. Through diligent planning, steady growth, and a heart open to God's leading, your business can stand for years—maybe even beyond your lifetime. You can leave behind an enterprise that continues blessing customers, employees, and the entire community.

Remember, longevity is not about clinging to the past or refusing change. It is about carrying forward unchanging truths—like honesty, empathy, and trust in God's care—into fresh approaches that keep your company vibrant. As you do this, you pass on a legacy that says: "With faith as our anchor, we stood strong in every storm. We served our customers, nurtured our team, and honored our Creator. And in doing so, we lived out a mission that endures."

So, step forward with confidence. Your faith-based business can be a long-burning light, guiding others, uplifting your neighborhood, and showcasing the power of blending timeless values with timely innovation. Each day, commit to your higher purpose, adapt as needed, and trust that God who began this good work in you will carry it to completion—through the decades ahead and into the hands of those who follow.

15

REFLECTIONS ON THE FAITH JOURNEY

"Remember the wonders He has done, His miracles, and the judgments He pronounced."

(1 CHRONICLES 16:12)

Looking Back on the Path of Faith

Every journey has a beginning, a middle, and an end—or at least a resting place before the next adventure begins. You started out with dreams, hopes, and maybe a bit of uncertainty about how your faith could guide you in building a business. Along the way, you encountered excitement, challenges, and lessons you never expected. Now, at this point, you pause to look back, gathering the treasures you found on the path.

This chapter is about reflecting on that journey—seeing how your faith has shaped you and your business from start to now. It is a chance to remember the obstacles that tested your resolve, the moments of grace that carried you forward, and the people who walked beside you. You will recall how each principle—from resilience to consistent prayer—helped you stand steady. And, as you reflect, you will gain fresh courage for whatever comes next.

Your journey is far from over, but this is a good spot to rest and notice how far you have come. Like a traveler who climbs a hill to view the road below, you can now see patterns and meanings that were hidden when you were in the thick of it. Perhaps you see that certain "accidents" were really blessings in disguise, or that your greatest trials taught you the best lessons. Your faith—like a faithful companion—remains with you, encouraging you to keep going. Let us explore the key reflections from this grand trek you have been on, trusting that you will find inspiration for the miles yet to travel.

Beginnings and Bold Steps

The Spark That Started It All

Do you remember the why behind your business? Maybe you felt a nudge in prayer, an idea in your heart that would not let go, or a desire to serve people in a way nobody else was doing. That spark might have seemed small—a seed of vision—but it lit a fire in you. Reflecting on it now reminds you that your enterprise was never only about profit. It was about answering a call, using your gifts, and living out your values in the marketplace.

Perhaps you started with a simple plan. You told a few friends about your dream, jotted down budget numbers, and prayed for direction. You hoped that, if God was indeed guiding you, doors would open. This sense of divine partnership can be incredibly motivating. In hindsight, you might see that even the slightest step of faith—like investing a small amount of money or renting a tiny office—was a courageous move. Never underestimate the power of those first, wobbly strides.

Overcoming Early Doubts

Starting something new can awaken doubts. "Am I strong enough? Smart enough? Do I truly have what it takes?" But if you look back at your initial days, you might recall how you wrestled with these fears, turning them over in prayer or talking them out with mentors. Maybe a verse or encouraging word gave you the courage to proceed. Now that you see the progress you have made, you realize that each doubt you faced became an opportunity to trust more deeply.

The Role of Encouragers

In those early stages, certain people likely cheered you on—family members, friends, a church group, or mentors who believed in your calling. They listened to your ideas, offered resources, or simply prayed for your success. Looking back, you can see how vital their support was. Their faith in you, alongside your faith in God, carried you past hurdles. Often, faith journeys are communal, not solitary. Reflecting on these encouragers sparks gratitude and reminds you of the support system that still surrounds you.

Trials That Tested Your Resolve

The Unseen Challenges

No matter how carefully you planned, obstacles appeared. Maybe you faced financial troubles, difficult hires, or personal crises that threatened to derail your progress. At times, you might have wondered if you took a wrong turn. But with each trial, you found a reservoir of inner strength. Your faith told you that no storm lasts forever and that you were not alone in facing it.

Reflecting now, you can see how these challenges shaped you. Perhaps they taught you patience, humility, or a clearer way to communicate. Problems often act like a mirror, showing us blind spots or weaknesses in our strategy. By dealing with them head-on, you grew more skilled and grounded. This growth is as much a part of your success story as any profit margin or new product launch.

Moments of Discouragement and Renewal

Discouragement can creep in quietly—after a string of slow sales, a nasty complaint, or a misstep in leadership. You might have felt tired, questioning if your vision was worth the trouble. Reflecting now, recall how you coped. Did you set aside time for prayer or quiet walks? Did you confide in a mentor or study Scripture that spoke hope into your weariness?

Often, it is in these valleys of discouragement that your faith becomes real and active. You discover that God's strength shows up when yours is running out. You also learn about perseverance—that gritty quality of pressing on, step by step, trusting that tomorrow can be better. Looking back, you might see these low points were actually turning points, leading you to fresh ideas or deeper convictions.

Lessons in Resilience

One major theme that emerges is resilience—the capacity to bounce back after each setback. Faith does not promise an easy path, but it assures you are not alone. When finances wobbled, you prayed for guidance and found an alternative revenue stream. When a key partner left, you leaned on other relationships or sought divine help to find someone new. Each bounce-back story, in hindsight, speaks of a stronger spirit than you realized you had. God's grace, along with your willingness to keep going, forged a resilience that still strengthens you today.

Surprises and Serendipities

Unexpected Doors

Sometimes, the best things happen unplanned. Perhaps you never thought you would expand to another state, but a random conversation opened that door. Or a major client stumbled upon your website through a friend's recommendation, igniting a new avenue of growth. Reflecting on these moments, you might see the hand of Providence weaving surprises into your story.

These "divine appointments" can remind you that while strategy and effort matter, there is also a bigger plan at work. Your faith helps you remain open to the unknown. Each time an unexpected door swung open, you likely felt both gratitude and wonder. These experiences underscore the idea that success is not only a result of your brilliance or hustle; sometimes, it is about being in the right place at the right time under God's orchestration.

Miracles in the Mundane

Not all surprises are big. Some are small blessings that show up in daily life—a supportive email arriving on a tough day, a helpful supplier giving you a discount, or a talented intern joining just when you needed extra help. When you slow down to reflect, you realize how many little miracles pepper your path. They might not make headlines, but they lift your spirit, reaffirming that your faith journey is sustained by countless pockets of grace.

Embracing the Unexpected

Reflecting on your story, you might notice that the most fruitful changes came when you let go of rigid plans and allowed faith to guide you. Maybe you pivoted your product line or changed your marketing approach. By staying flexible and open to new ideas, you discovered better outcomes. Faith fosters humility—a readiness to say, "I do not know everything, but I trust that if I listen closely, I will find the next right step." This humility paves the way for creative leaps and unexpected growth.

Spiritual Growth Through the Journey

Drawing Closer to God

Running a faith-based business is not just about external results. It can also deepen your personal relationship with God. Reflecting now, you might see how each challenge brought you to your knees in prayer. Over time, this built a habit of daily communication with the divine. You learned to seek guidance not only for big decisions but also for small steps, such as how to resolve a team conflict or how to word a social media post with grace.

You may also have experienced moments of worship within your work—feeling awe when a project came together beautifully, or gratitude when someone thanked you for changing their life. These glimpses remind you that all creation, including commerce, can be an arena for divine activity.

Lessons in Character

Business can be a training ground for virtues like patience, honesty, and kindness. Maybe you used to struggle with impatience, snapping at slow progress. Or you were tempted to cut corners in a contract. But as you stayed alert to faith's moral standards, you chose the higher path, refining your character over time. These internal changes—though less visible than revenue charts—are deeply significant. They shape who you are, making you a more trustworthy leader, friend, or mentor.

Strengthening Trust

Faith often involves trusting what you cannot see. In business, that can mean launching a product not fully knowing how customers will respond, or stepping out with a new partnership even if it feels risky. Each time you took such a leap and saw it work out (or learned from it if it did not), your trust in God's provision grew. Now, looking back, you see how these steps formed a tapestry of trust, each thread reinforcing the next.

Influencing Others Through Your Journey

Inspiring Team Members

As you reflect, consider the employees or partners who witnessed your faith in action. They saw you handle stress with prayer, treat conflicts with compassion, and own up to mistakes with humility. This lifestyle can leave a powerful impression. Some may have become more open to spiritual questions themselves or started embracing virtues like honesty and generosity. Even those who do not share your beliefs often respect consistency and genuine care.

Touching Customers' Lives

Your customers might have felt something different about your brand—like a warmth or authenticity that is missing from many businesses. Maybe they left your shop feeling encouraged, not just sold to. Or they discovered that your after-sale support included a personal touch, making them loyal fans. By letting your faith shape your customer interactions, you provided more than a product or service. You offered a glimpse of something deeper—a reflection of a God who cares for every detail in our lives.

Creating a Ripple Effect

Faithful actions often have ripple effects beyond what you see. A supplier impressed by your ethics might adopt fair practices in their own deals. A family member might decide to pursue a dream because your example showed them it was possible. A local charity might receive help from your profits or volunteer work, further touching others' lives. Reflecting on these ripples encourages you to keep living your values, knowing that each small act of integrity can grow into bigger transformations down the line.

Continuing the Faith Journey

Embracing the Unfinished Story

Your reflection does not mark an ending. It is a checkpoint, reminding you that your story is still unfolding. Faith teaches that life is a pilgrimage—we keep learning, evolving, and drawing closer to God as long as we have breath. Perhaps you have fresh ideas or expansions in mind, or you feel led to mentor new entrepreneurs. Looking back at your journey so far can guide you on how to move forward wisely.

Staying True to Your Principles

As your business grows, temptations might arise to cut corners or forget the original mission. Maybe bigger competitors push you to slash wages or hide fees. Reflection helps you remember why you started, encouraging you to keep faith at the center, no matter how large or complex your enterprise becomes. Even if you pivot directions, your moral and spiritual framework remains your guiding star.

Remaining Teachable

No one is too experienced to learn. Faith-based leaders keep a teachable spirit, aware that new challenges will demand new skills and deeper trust. You might sign up for courses to refine your management style, invite a spiritual mentor to keep you accountable, or join a mastermind group with fellow business owners who share your beliefs. This humility and willingness to learn keeps your heart open to God's surprises and corrections.

Practical Exercises for Ongoing Reflection

Journaling Regularly

Even after finishing this chapter, continue writing your thoughts down weekly or monthly. Summarize victories, frustrations, and spiritual insights. By creating a consistent record, you can revisit it whenever you feel lost or discouraged, seeing how God guided you before. This practice cultivates a heart of gratitude and keeps your lessons fresh in mind.

Prayer Walks or Retreats

Take occasional breaks—a day-long retreat or a short prayer walk in nature—to pray, read Scripture, or just be silent. Ask yourself: "Where am I now? Where do I feel led? Are there areas where I have drifted from my values?" Let the stillness reveal any course corrections. Sometimes, stepping away from daily bustle allows the Holy Spirit to whisper guidance you cannot hear when you are rushed.

Sharing Your Testimony

Openly sharing your business testimony can bless others. Whether it is at a church group, a civic club, or a conference, telling how faith shaped your journey can encourage someone struggling in their own path. Prepare a brief outline: your dream, the trials, the lessons, and the ongoing trust that sustains you. Hearing real-life faith stories has a unique power to stir hope in listeners.

Encouragement for the Road Ahead

Give Yourself Grace

Reflecting on the past, you may see areas where you wish you had done better. Perhaps you regret a broken partnership or a missed opportunity. Let your faith remind you of grace—both from God and, hopefully, from those affected. Forgive yourself, learn from mistakes, and move forward with fresh resolve. Perfection is not the goal; growth is.

Remember the Big Picture

Yes, business must handle practical matters like bills, products, and marketing. But do not lose sight of the bigger reason you ventured out on this path. If your faith calls you to serve people, uplift communities, or bring light into dark places, keep that mission at the forefront. This perspective injects passion into daily tasks and helps you handle setbacks with serenity.

Celebrate Ongoing Progress

Reflections are not just about the past. They also highlight how far you have come and the steps you continue to take. Make it a habit to celebrate milestones—quarterly goals, new hires who share your values, or small changes that align the business more with your faith. These celebrations create a climate of joy that encourages everyone to keep striving.

Real-Life Tales of Continued Growth

The Family Business That Reinvented Itself

A family-run store stood for forty years in a small town. Each generation faced new trials—like chain stores moving in. Yet, each time, they adapted by leaning on prayer and seeking fresh ideas. One generation switched to specialty items; another launched online shipping. Throughout it all, the core remained: serving customers like neighbors. Their story, told through local media, shows how faith and reflection keep a business heart alive across decades.

The Mission-Driven Tech Startup

A tech startup aimed to solve real social problems, such as bridging communication gaps for people with disabilities. Years later, after some major product flops and near-bankruptcy, the founders refused to give up. They prayed, recalibrated their approach, and found a workable model by partnering with nonprofits. Now, they are stable and still pushing for new innovations. Regular reflection helped them see which efforts aligned with their spiritual mission and which were just distractions.

The Mentor Who Empowers Others

A successful entrepreneur, known for her faith-based approach, decided her legacy would not be another product line but a mentorship network for aspiring businesswomen. She reflected on her journey and saw how mentors had shaped her. Now, she invests time guiding younger leaders, teaching them about ethics, stewardship, and service. Her reflection on her own path fuels her passion to raise up others, ensuring that the flame of faith-driven enterprise continues to burn brightly.

Continuing Forward with Hope

Your story is still unfolding. You have traveled through the hills and valleys of starting, sustaining, and growing a faith-based business. You have tasted both triumphs and trials, and through it all, your faith has been a companion, sometimes a pillar of strength, sometimes a gentle whisper urging you onward. Reflecting on the past chapters, you see how each principle—like resilience, daily devotion, humility, celebrating small wins, and learning from failure—plays a part in forming a tapestry of grace and determination.

As you stand here, looking back and then ahead, remember that reflection is not a one-time event. It is a habit—an ongoing conversation with yourself, your team, and God, asking: "How are we doing? Are we still on course with our mission? What might we do differently?" This habit of reflection keeps your business and your spirit alive, preventing stagnation and reminding you of your higher calling.

Keep your eyes open for divine surprises. Keep your heart soft to lessons hidden in setbacks. Keep your resolve to serve others, trusting that in doing so, you honor both your customers and your Creator. Let your reflections spark gratitude for all that has been and hope for all that will be. And let this moment of pause fill you with renewed passion, so that tomorrow you return to your work with a clear mind, a trusting heart, and the faith that the best chapters of your journey may be yet to come.

WHERE TO GO FROM HERE

Standing at a Crossroads

You have come a long way, exploring how faith can shape your mindset, guide your decisions, and fuel your resilience in business. Perhaps you feel inspired, full of new ideas about running a venture that honors both God and the people you serve. Or maybe you sense you have only scratched the surface and wonder, "Where do I go next?"

This chapter is about next steps. You stand at a crossroads, having gathered insights and tools for building a faith-based business. Now it is time to put them into action, shaping your plans for tomorrow. We will look at practical ways to continue growing, ways to deepen your faith-entrepreneurial skills, and methods to keep your heart aligned with your higher calling. Think of this as your roadmap for transforming everything you have learned so far into a living, breathing journey.

You might already have an existing business, or you might just be starting out. Either way, the principles remain the same: keep your faith close, stay humble, and take steps that reflect your values. This chapter will outline how to keep moving forward without losing momentum. You will discover how to stay accountable, how to serve others more effectively, and how to dream even bigger while staying true to the core lessons you have embraced. Let us set off on this new stage of the journey, trusting that the same grace that brought you here will guide you to where you are meant to go next.

Revisit Your Foundations

Reviewing Your Core Vision and Values

Before rushing into fresh tasks, pause to review the mission statement or faith-based goals you set earlier. Maybe you wrote a short paragraph explaining why you started the business and how you hoped to serve. Or perhaps you only had a rough mental picture. Now is a good time to refine it. Ask yourself:

- Does this mission still ring true in my heart?
- Have I seen aspects of it change or expand?
- Are there any parts that need updating?

Adjusting your vision is not a sign of failure. It simply means you have grown. Sometimes, after months or years of practical experience, you see more clearly what God has placed on your heart. Rewriting or reaffirming your vision keeps you anchored, ensuring that the next steps you take still align with the deeper purpose that first inspired you.

Checking in with Your Values

It is also wise to reflect on your core values—such as honesty, generosity, compassion, or stewardship. How well are these values woven into your daily operations? Have you noticed any drift away from them? For instance, maybe you realize your busy schedule led you to cut corners in communication. Or perhaps you have found that your pricing strategy no longer reflects your goal of fairness.

A simple exercise is to list your main values and rate how your business practices match each one. Then brainstorm ways to better embody them. This can mean updating policies, rethinking how you treat customers, or encouraging your team to adopt new behaviors. By making course corrections now, you lay a stronger foundation for future growth.

Embracing the Lessons Learned

Reflection often reveals lessons about what works and what does not. Maybe you learned that your morning prayer time truly sets the tone for your day. Or that resilience grew each time you celebrated small wins with your team. These lessons are not just memories; they are tools for your future success. Commit to integrating them. For example, if consistent prayer or journaling helped you handle stress, schedule it into your routine. If a certain marketing style flopped, change it. Moving forward starts with applying the insights you have already gained.

Setting New Goals and Strategies

Dreaming Bigger (but Wisely)

Your faith journey may have sparked fresh dreams: launching a new product line, opening a second location, or serving a different customer base. God might nudge your heart to step into a new area of influence. How do you turn these dreams into reality?

Start by writing them down. Then break each dream into smaller steps, much like you did when you first began. For example, if you dream of exporting your goods to another country, research shipping costs and regulations as a first step. If you want to open a new branch, study the local market. This method keeps your big vision from feeling overwhelming while maintaining a sense of direction.

Creating an Action Plan

To keep momentum, create a short-term and long-term plan. Short-term goals might cover the next three to six months—like improving your website, hiring one new team member, or boosting your social media presence. Long-term goals could stretch one to three years, involving major expansions or brand transformations.

Ensure each goal aligns with the core values you just revisited. For instance, if generosity is a key value, plan how you will use new revenue to give back to your community. Maybe set a goal: "When we reach X amount of monthly profit, we will donate Y percentage to a local charity." Tying your business achievements to acts of service ensures your faith remains woven into your strategies.

Balancing Faith and Practicality

Faith invites you to dream with hope, but it also calls for practical stewardship of resources. As you set your next goals, ask, "Is this financially wise? Do I have the time and team to manage this expansion?" Pray for discernment. Sometimes, a door might seem appealing but is not truly the path God wants you to take. Other times, a door might scare you, but the Holy Spirit encourages you to push forward. Balancing faith and good sense protects you from both reckless leaps and timid avoidance of growth.

Accountability and Community

Finding Mentors and Peers

One of the best moves you can make is to seek accountability from mentors or fellow believers in business. Why? Because going it alone can lead to blind spots, isolation, and burnout. Mentors who share your values can offer advice, keep you honest, and remind you to stay grounded in your faith. A supportive peer group—like a small mastermind of faith-driven entrepreneurs—can provide fresh ideas and encourage you when challenges loom.

Search for networks online or ask around your church or community. Some mentors may be local, while others can connect via video calls. Once you have found a mentor or group, schedule regular check-ins to discuss your progress, brainstorm solutions, and pray together. This fellowship often energizes your journey, ensuring you never feel you are fighting battles alone.

Team Leadership and Growth

If you have employees, now is a good time to deepen their engagement. Communicate your updated vision and involve them in planning. Encourage them to bring ideas on how to reflect faith-based values in daily work—like more transparent communication or volunteer activities. Offer training opportunities. When employees see themselves as part of something bigger, they become allies rather than just workers.

Also, consider whether any team member is ready for leadership roles. Grooming new leaders spreads the load and cultivates a legacy of faith-driven leadership. Give them projects that challenge them to apply spiritual principles (like compassion or honesty) in real business tasks. This approach fosters a culture where everyone grows together, united by shared values.

Staying Open to Feedback

Accountability also involves listening to feedback from customers, the community, or your own family. If someone points out you have drifted from your core principles or overlooked a group's needs, do not be defensive. Instead, see it as God possibly using them to guide you back on track. By humbly accepting criticism (when valid) and making changes, you keep your integrity strong and your relationships healthy.

Serving and Outreach

New Ways to Serve Your Community

A faith-based business is more than its sales; it is a channel for good. So, as you move forward, explore fresh outreach possibilities. If you already sponsor a local charity, maybe you can deepen that partnership or invite customers to join in. If you have only ever supported one cause, consider branching out—could you organize a community clean-up, offer free workshops, or mentor at-risk youth?

Ask God to show you unmet needs in your town or the markets you serve. You might discover a local school needing donated supplies, a homeless shelter short on volunteers, or a small nonprofit lacking modern tech. By offering your resources or expertise, you express your faith tangibly, building goodwill and a sense of shared purpose.

Telling Your Community Story

Each new act of service can also connect you more deeply with customers who share your heart for making a difference. Let them know about your community efforts, not as a boast, but as an invitation to join. You can post updates on social media, create events, or write short blog posts about the impact. People often admire businesses that invest in their neighborhood. This loyalty can also expand your customer base.

However, ensure your service remains sincere. Avoid using charity just to look good. The difference between genuine kindness and a marketing trick is huge. Customers and community members can sense authenticity. Approach service as an overflow of your faith, with any positive publicity being a welcome, but secondary, benefit.

Expanding Impact Through Partnerships

Another idea is to collaborate with other faith-based or socially conscious businesses. Together, you can host bigger events or pool resources for greater impact. For instance, a local café might partner with a clothing store to organize a coat drive in winter, or a restaurant might team up with a tech company to sponsor a charity run. Such partnerships not only multiply your outreach efforts but also introduce your brand to new audiences. Jointly shining as lights in the marketplace, you create a brighter, more welcoming community.

Continuing Personal and Spiritual Growth

Ongoing Faith Practices

As your business grows, do not abandon the spiritual routines that anchored you—like morning devotion, Scripture study, or prayer walks. In fact, you may need them even more amid busier schedules. Building a consistent practice—such as a daily or weekly quiet time— helps you stay connected to God's voice. Keeping that line of communication open protects you from drifting into purely human-driven ambition.

Some leaders host optional devotion times for their team, though this depends on your workplace culture. If that is too formal, you could simply encourage those who wish to begin the day with a moment of silence or reflection. The key is: spiritual growth does not happen by accident. You must carve out space to nurture it, just as you would any important business task.

Education and Skill-Building

Faith calls us to stewardship of our talents. That includes sharpening your business know-how. Seek out resources—books, podcasts, or courses—that explore topics like ethical leadership, marketing, or financial management from a faith perspective. If you notice a personal weakness (like conflict resolution or public speaking), find a mentor or sign up for a class. Each new skill can help you serve clients better and lead your team more effectively.

You might also explore faith-centered business conferences or retreats. These events let you network with others who share your convictions. Hearing speakers who overcame challenges with God's help can inspire you to aim higher and think more creatively. Do not be afraid to invest time and money into your personal growth; a better-equipped you means a more stable enterprise for everyone involved.

Emotional and Mental Well-Being

Finally, do not overlook your emotional health. Running a faith-based business can be demanding, as you juggle spiritual ideals with worldly pressures. Anxiety, burnout, or discouragement can creep in. If you sense you are wearing thin, reach out for help. Talk to a counselor, pastor, or confidant. Develop stress-management habits, whether that is exercise, journaling, or sharing burdens in prayer groups. A healthy mind and heart enable you to continue blessing others without losing yourself.

Innovations and Next Steps in Marketing

Fresh Ways to Connect with Customers

As your company matures, keep your marketing approaches updated. Platforms and trends shift rapidly—what worked last year might be less effective now. If you used to rely on in-person events, consider digital tools. If you have a solid social media presence, maybe experiment with short, uplifting video clips or interactive webinars. Faith can guide the tone of your marketing, ensuring it stays honest, uplifting, and respectful. Look for creative angles that highlight your commitment to service and integrity.

Storytelling with Faith

Customers love authentic stories—about how your brand started, lessons you learned, or the people you have helped along the way. Could you feature mini-testimonies from employees or clients who have been impacted by your business's faith-driven approach? Could you film a short behind-the-scenes video showing how a product is made with prayerful attention to detail? Such storytelling can be powerful, but be genuine. Overdoing or exaggerating can backfire. Aim to share glimpses of real faith in action, not staged scenes.

Reaching New Markets

Maybe you started locally but sense that it is time to reach a regional or even international audience. Research carefully, respecting cultural differences and local laws. Faith teaches us to honor people from various backgrounds. Adapting your product or communication style might be necessary without sacrificing core beliefs. If your brand is known for positivity and ethics, those qualities can resonate with diverse groups as you expand. Just ensure you have the infrastructure—like reliable shipping or bilingual support—to handle a broader scope.

Anticipating Challenges with Confidence

Preparing for Economic Ups and Downs

Business cycles can be unpredictable—recessions, currency fluctuations, or sudden inflation can test your resilience. By keeping an emergency fund or alternative revenue stream, you guard against panic. Faith encourages you to trust God's provision, but it also calls you to wisdom in planning. If times get lean, lean on prayer for calm and rely on your team's creativity. Sometimes, downturns spark fresh innovations that strengthen your business for the long run.

Handling Competitor Pressures

As you succeed, competitors may take notice. Some might try to copy your offerings or outdo you in price. Do not let anxiety drive you to compromise on ethics or rush into price wars. Return to prayer, seek creative solutions, and focus on serving customers with excellence. In many cases, the loyalty you have built through integrity and kindness cannot be easily duplicated by a rival. It takes time and moral consistency to earn such a reputation.

Navigating Leadership Transitions

There may come a day when you sense God leading you to step back or hand the reins to someone else. Whether that transition is years away or looming soon, plan for it. Train successors, document processes, and ensure your faith-based principles are clearly stated. If you wait until an emergency forces you to leave abruptly, confusion can hurt the business. But a thoughtful exit plan, guided by prayer, can keep the enterprise stable and your mission intact long after you are gone.

Celebrating Milestones and Growth

Marking Key Achievements

As you move forward, do not forget to pause and celebrate. When you reach a milestone—such as hiring your 10th employee or hitting a certain sales goal—acknowledge the moment with gratitude. This could be a small office party, a social media post thanking your supporters, or a personal prayer of thanks. Celebrations keep morale high and remind everyone of the progress achieved through faith and collaboration.

Sharing Success with the Community

If God blesses you with growth, let it benefit those around you. Offer job opportunities to local people, invest in improving your neighborhood, or donate to a cause close to your heart. Let your success become a reason to bless others, not a source of personal pride. By sharing your abundance, you fulfill the spiritual principle of caring for the weak and uplifting the community. This cycle of giving builds even stronger bonds with customers who see your business as a force for good.

Continual Thanksgiving

One hallmark of a faith-based business is constant gratitude—thanking God for each win, big or small. Even if your milestones are modest—like finishing a tough project or resolving a customer complaint smoothly—an attitude of thanks keeps you humble. It reminds you that your talents and resources ultimately come from a higher source. This sense of gratitude colors how you view both success and failure, creating a peaceful, hopeful atmosphere in your company.

Long-Term Vision and Legacy

Envisioning the Future

Picture your business in five, ten, or twenty years. If you remain faithful to your calling, what might it look like? More locations? A stronger online presence? Or perhaps you focus on depth—like deepening relationships with a smaller group of loyal customers. There is no single correct path, only the one that aligns with your mission and capabilities. Allow yourself to dream, then ask God to refine and direct those dreams.

Preparing the Next Generation

If you have children or younger relatives, they might one day take over. Consider how to introduce them to the company's faith-driven ethos. Let them watch how you make decisions, especially tough ones, showing them that faith guides you rather than pure profit. If they do not wish to take over, that is fine too; you can look for a trusted partner or an employee who shares your heart. The key is intentional planning so your legacy does not vanish if you step away.

Eternal Impact

Ultimately, your faith-based enterprise is temporary in the grand timeline. However, the impact on people's hearts and lives can last forever. Reflect on how you can weave eternal values into every part of your work. Perhaps you sponsor a Bible study or prayer meeting for those interested, offer counseling to employees in need, or produce items that carry messages of hope. These small touches can change lives in ways that outlive any brand. Keeping eternity in mind helps you stay true to what matters most.

Where to go from here?

The question "Where to go from here?" echoes through every season of business. After all you have learned, you now have a clearer sense of direction. You know how to revisit your values, set fresh goals, maintain accountability, serve others, and keep growing both spiritually and practically. Each principle you have embraced—from resilience in hard times to celebrating small wins—becomes an ingredient in your ongoing recipe for success.

The torch is in your hands. A faith-based business is a living story, with each chapter shaped by your willingness to trust God, put in honest work, and uplift those around you. By following the steps in this chapter—revisiting foundations, creating new strategies, building accountability networks, and continuing to serve—you move forward with confidence. You do not walk blindly; you have a roadmap of faith and experience guiding your steps.

Remember, the journey is not always smooth. You will likely encounter fresh challenges. But with each challenge comes an opportunity to deepen your faith and sharpen your skills. Let this be your encouragement: You are equipped, you are called, and you are not alone. Continue to lean on the One who planted the dream in your heart. In doing so, you will keep your business on a path of integrity, purpose, and lasting impact. May your next steps overflow with blessings—both for you and for everyone you touch along the way.

ABOUT THE AUTHOR

From the time he launched his first lawn-mowing service at age fourteen, Carl B. Johnson has been captivated by the power of entrepreneurship. Over the years, he's started and grown multiple ventures, learning firsthand how faith can transform a simple idea into a meaningful, purposeful business. Through highs and lows, Carl remained committed to weaving biblical principles into every decision, believing that real success begins with service, integrity, and a humble spirit.

Today, he shares what he's learned—both the early mistakes and the later breakthroughs—so that others can experience the benefits of running a faith-anchored enterprise. Alongside speaking engagements and mentorship roles, Carl continues to explore new ways of blending spiritual insight with real-world strategy. Whether he's at his office desk, on a volunteer project in the community, or spending time with family, Carl is always on the lookout for moments when faith sparks innovation. This book is the culmination of his life's work, an invitation to build a legacy that goes beyond profit and reflects the heart of a greater purpose.

Made in the USA
Columbia, SC
01 March 2025

54549521R00137